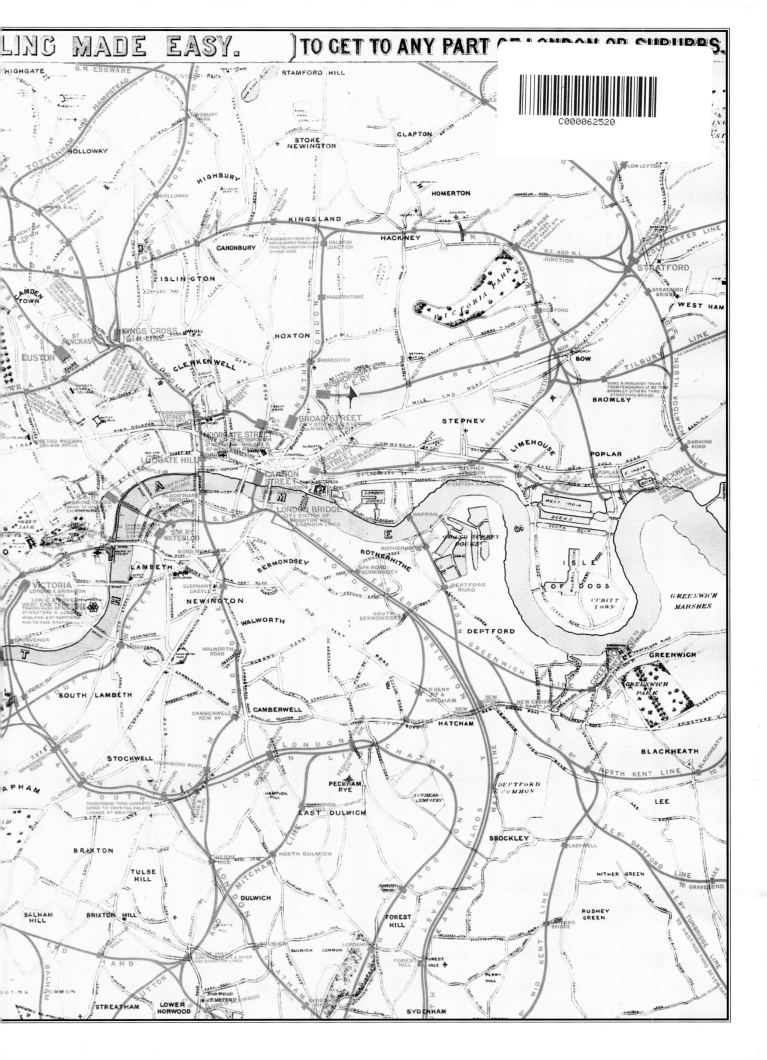

Railways
in and around
London
Then & Now

REFRESHMENT FACILITIES

GREAT HALL — CAFETERIA & BUFFET

PLATFORM 13 — BUFFET

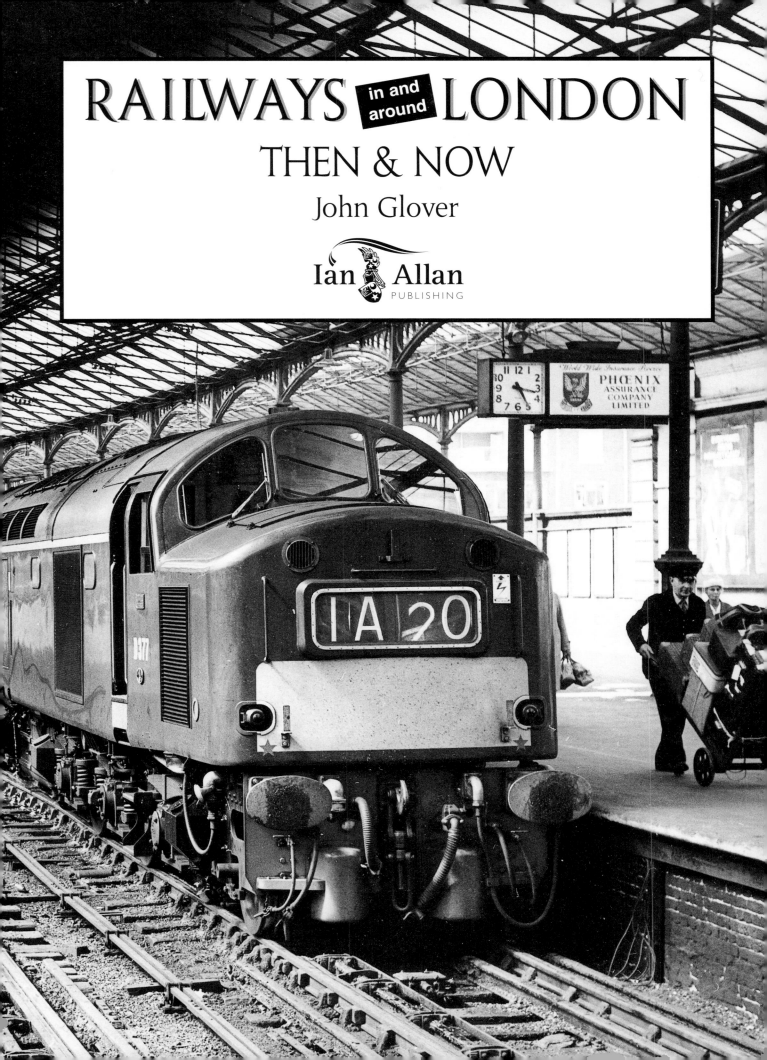

RAILWAYS in and around LONDON
THEN & NOW
John Glover

Ian Allan
PUBLISHING

Contents

Half title page:
GERRARDS CROSS

Then: 13 September 1979
Even at this stage, this was the only passenger train to take the old Great Western main line from Banbury to Paddington via High Wycombe. An unidentified Class 47 passes at speed with the 06.45 from Birmingham New Street.

Now: 12 November 1998
Changes at Gerrards Cross have reduced the running lines to two, with the result that the down loop is now the down line and the down fast is the up line. This has meant considerable work in moving the up platform and ensuring that the running lines do not have a pronounced kink in them! Further work has created a turnback siding and more car parking. No 165008 forms the 11.17 Marylebone to Aylesbury. *Author (2)*

Title page:
EUSTON

Then: 1962
The arrivals side at the old Euston, or the lowest numbered platforms, was the natural objective for the meeters and greeters. This was adjacent to a modest 'arrivals bureau', where screens displayed expected times of arrival in a darkened room which had reasonably comfortable seats... In this picture, Class 40 diesel No D337 is in Platform 1 with a train of mixed BR and LMS stock; with the glazed roof, this view sums up the old Euston admirably.

Now: 20 October 1998
North Western Trains' No 158759 stands in the adjacent Platform 2, following arrival with the 06.27 from Blackpool North/06.43 from Rochdale. The environment typifies today's Euston. *Brian Stephenson/Author*

Acknowledgements

I should like to acknowledge the ready help of Derek Mercer in producing many of the photographic prints used in the book. Photographers are credited individually.

I am also much indebted to David Penrose of FWT, whose assistance in tracing the map of 1870 and permitting its reproduction on the endpapers greatly enhance the contents of this volume.

As always, the series of Track Diagrams produced by the Quail Map Co is of great value in sorting out the minutiae of railway layouts, and Douglas Rose's Diagrammatic History of the London Underground provides a comprehensive record of the evolution of that organisation.

First published 1999

ISBN 0 7110 2671 8

Published by Ian Allan Publishing

an imprint of Ian Allan Publishing Ltd, Terminal House, Shepperton, Surrey TW17 8AS.
Printed by Ian Allan Printing Ltd, Riverdene Business Park, Hersham, Surrey KT12 4RG.

Code: 9907/A3

TONBRIDGE

Then: 16 October 1978

The Hastings loading gauge restrictions resulted in diesel-electric units of no more than 2.5m wide. This happens to coincide with the maximum permitted width of buses and coaches in the UK, but is much less than these units' contemporaries which were about 2.818m in width. Class 202 set No 1011 was one of the longer frame variety, seen here arriving from Hastings at Platform 2. Although apparently tight, this bridge is able to accommodate ordinary stock.

Now: 21 September 1998

The limitations of the British loading gauge apply to all trains that may run on it, and this included Eurostar. An up Eurostar working is seen at the same location, and although it is using the adjoining arch, the design limitations imposed are clear. *Author (2)*

Introduction

This book sets out to show how the railway in the London area has changed physically over time. With pictures from many sources, but principally the Ian Allan library and the author's own photographs and his collection, the illustrations have been selected to highlight change, or sometimes the lack of it.

Generally, the same location has been used, when available, for the 'then' and the 'now' shots. However, the author has tried to adopt a reasonably creative approach, since many pictures in which the train is dominant tell one little about the location. Photographic viewpoints for the 'now' work have been selected to try and convey a feeling of place wherever possible, and in some cases this means that the train occupies a relatively small portion of the total picture area. Sometimes, obstructions of one sort or another limit the present-day views available. The unrestrained growth of lineside vegetation is one such obstacle, while the use of close mesh security fencing, particularly on London Underground, is another hazard for the photographer.

When this book was first being discussed, the geographical area which it should cover gave rise to considerable thought. The boundaries of Greater London seemed a little too constrained, while those of the former Network SouthEast were clearly much too wide. The intention was to cover lines which depended for their existence on the capital, but to exclude those where London traffic was of rather lesser importance.

The area covered includes railways up to 30 or so miles from central London, in a wide arc which encompasses Southend, Luton, Maidenhead, Guildford and Tonbridge. This includes the whole of London Underground, the Docklands Light Railway and Croydon Tramlink.

The presentation follows the same order as the Great Britain Passenger Railway Timetable, produced nowadays by Railtrack. Starting with the London, Tilbury & Southend line on the north bank of the Thames, the progression is anticlockwise from there round to the South Eastern & Chatham, after which it is followed by London Underground and the light rail systems. However, the basis is the individual routes of the pre-1923 companies, rather than that of today's Train Operating Companies.

Today, there are 25 passenger train companies nationally which provide regular scheduled services available to the public. All these have agreements with the Franchising Director. In addition, there are Eurostar and Heathrow Express. Of the 27, only five do not run services to London. The London termini at which each of these companies may be found are listed in Appendix I.

The 'now' photography for this volume was carried out mostly in the autumn of 1998. Many of the new train liveries were in evidence, but often perhaps in lesser proportions than might have been anticipated.

Friends have helped to identify photographic locations where details on the backs of prints are sparse, or sometimes completely lacking. One may have one's suspicions as to the location represented in the picture, but harder information is needed to attribute a print, let alone find the place in real life! I have estimated dates in the style 'c19xx' for those pictures which bear no such indications.

John Glover
Worcester Park
March 1999

London Railway Development

Early Years

London has been a focus of railway operations, ever since the railway grew beyond its formative stage when it was solely an adjunct to industrial production. The first true main line railway to arrive in London was the London & Birmingham at Euston in 1837, followed in quick succession by Brunel's Great Western to Bishop's Road, Paddington in 1838 and the London & Southampton to Nine Elms, also in 1838.

Essentially, these were main line railways. More local affairs consisted of the London & Greenwich of 1836 (London Bridge and, originally, Deptford) and the London & Croydon Railway (1839). North of the river, the Eastern Counties started operations from Mile End Road to Romford in 1839 and the London & Blackwall Railway from Fenchurch Street in 1841. Also in east London, the Northern & Eastern Railway opened its line from Stratford along the Lea Valley as far as Broxbourne in 1840.

In 1850, the Great Northern opened its line from the original Maiden Lane terminus to Peterborough. In the short space of 15 years or so, most of the major players among the main line railway companies had been established. Already, though, it was possible to detect some of the developments which would take place.

The major railways had not been able to position themselves in the centre of London. The capital city was already just that; quite apart from what today would be termed environmental considerations, land acquisition was costly. So the railway companies had to make do with second best, placing their termini on the then outskirts. The London & Southampton Railway's Nine Elms terminus was quickly found to be too far from central London, and the extension to Waterloo replaced Nine Elms in 1848.

Royal Commission

Parliament was concerned that excessive railway infrastructure would end up dominating London. A Royal Commission on London Termini was set up in 1846, and charged with reporting on the issue. Broadly, the RCLT confirmed that the then existing situation north of the river, with termini dotted along the present Euston Road and its continuations, should remain. On the south bank, railways should be allowed, provided they did not cross the Thames to the north bank.

Such further surface railway construction within the central area that did take place was largely on the grounds of benefits in reducing street traffic congestion. A later reason was to allow railways to serve the London wholesale markets. Thus came

EUSTON

Then: 6 June 1957
The monumental scale of Philip Hardwick's Doric Arch at Euston is plainly evident in this view. That it was demolished a few years later is perhaps to be regretted, whatever the operational benefits to the new Euston which ensued. *Ian Allan Library*

Now: 1 September 1998
London Underground chose the Doric Arch as a decoration for the tiling in its new Victoria line platforms, opened in 1968. One wonders how many of today's passengers recognise the tiles for what they represent. *Author*

Now: 23 July 1992
'Of all his works it is, we may be certain, by the old main line from London to Bristol that he would wish to be remembered.' Thus wrote L. T. C. Rolt in his 1957 biography of Isambard Kingdom Brunel, 1806-59, whose statue guarded the entrance from the Lawn to the Underground at Paddington. This area of the station is presently being redeveloped, and it is to be hoped that a suitable site will be found for its display subsequently. *Author*

Now: 20 October 1998
The former hotel which graces the front of St Pancras is certainly a distinctive and memorable building. Opinions on its merits follow the vagaries of fashion, but we can be thankful that it was not demolished in the 1970s as once seemed likely. *Author*

about the construction of the Widened Lines through the present King's Cross Thameslink to Moorgate and the route from north to south via the Snow Hill tunnel and Blackfriars railway bridge.

West End or City?

Another problem was the breadth of London; the distance of the central area from east to west is around four miles, or about twice that from Euston Road to the Thames. Thus London Bridge may be a suitable location from which to reach the City, but how was the passenger to get to the West End? Euston was more centrally placed, though this could be construed as being convenient for neither. On the other hand, Paddington — at a time when the City was of greater importance than the yet to be fully developed West End — was very much out on a limb.

This led to the need for dual termini; thus the Midland's St Pancras was supplemented (indeed, it was actually preceded) by services to Moorgate via the Widened Lines. Similarly, the Brighton's Victoria had its city counterpart in the (slightly) lower level station at London Bridge. The South Eastern Railway gained access to Charing Cross for the West End as well as Cannon Street and London Bridge for the City. The SER was one of the few companies to get round the Royal Commission's recommendations, although both extensions were very costly exercises.

The third issue was the nature of the traffics carried. In mid-Victorian London, the docks in the East End were of great importance for freight, but passenger commuting in the volumes which we know today was still for the future. Docks access for the railways was needed and was provided. However, it was those railway companies that served parts of the country without minerals or heavy industry, and derived most of their revenues from agriculture and passengers, which did the most to stimulate the passenger businesses. Essentially, these were the companies serving the areas south of the Thames, and to the east and northeast. It is the swathe of termini from Waterloo round to Liverpool Street which then, as now, carried the bulk of commuter traffic. The Great Northern, serving King's Cross, Broad Street and Moorgate was perhaps the watershed company. Railways which had access to the industrial heartlands of Britain had more profitable traffics on which to devote managerial time.

This did not stop the railways from forming extensive networks outside the central area, and in this the lines such as the North London and West London were of particular importance. These lines connected up the radial lines from the capital, and provided routes over which freight traffic in particular could be transferred between them. The original concept of interchange referred to freight. In most of the essentials, the railway system by mid-Victorian times can be related closely to that of today.

The Role of the Underground

All this activity still left the centre of London largely unserved by rail. Here was a role for the underground railway, met initially by the cut-and-cover of subsurface lines from 1863 onwards with the Metropolitan and then the (Metropolitan) District Railway. Thus Great Western passengers could at last reach the City via a steam-hauled railway which ran beneath that same Euston Road.

But the disruption caused during construction was enormous, and there were huge difficulties for subsurface railways in crossing natural obstacles such as watercourses. The Metropolitan and the District did manage to complete a circumferential route around the central area by 1884 (today's Circle Line), with many branches.

The creation of the deep level tube railways came later, with the inauguration of the City & South London Railway in 1890. By the end of the Edwardian era central London tube construction was all but complete. From 1898, London & South Western passengers were able to reach Bank through the Waterloo & City Line, and this was followed by the Central London Railway (1900) and the Yerkes tubes which formed the genesis of today's Bakerloo, Northern and Piccadilly Lines (1906/7). In retrospect, this was an amazing achievement in a period of less than 20 years. It was not until the Victoria Line was built in 1968-72 that the central area network was again expanded.

The splendid map (reproduced on the endpapers) is dated 24 May 1870, and includes all railways then in existence. This was in the very early days of the Underground, represented by the Metropolitan and the (Metropolitan) District Railways only. The Circle Line had yet to be completed, and the first line of the deep level tube railway was still two decades away. Overall, it is decidedly familiar, although some connections then available no longer exist.

The Spread of London

By the end of the Edwardian era, the Underground in the central area had reached a state of completion, for the time being. But this still left plenty of scope for expansion outwards, and this went hand in hand with the creation of what is so accurately described by Alan A. Jackson in his book *Semi-Detached London*. Outwards the Underground went.

In the suburbs, new considerations arose. Speculative network extensions into areas which it was hoped would be developed for housing helped provide traffic for the Underground. Much of the trackwork was on the surface rather than in tunnel. The resulting revenues would also help to defray the costs incurred in tunnelling in the central area. Tunnelling north of the Thames through London clay was straightforward, whereas south of the river the more difficult water-bearing sands and gravels were encountered. However, the attitude of the main line railways also changed. To the north and west, the main lines affected at least a degree of indifference, but elsewhere as related passenger traffic became a railway company's main livelihood. The net result has been that little more than one tenth of the stations served by London Underground are south of the Thames.

The corollary was that electrification, which reduced production costs and resulted also in a more attractive service to the public, could also be good for the main line railways. Local traffics, even south of the Thames, were now being abstracted to a serious extent by the newfangled electric trams.

On the main line railways, consolidation was undertaken with the Grouping of 1923. In the London area, the Southern Railway was very active in progressing the business case for electrification, and then undertaking it. This was the contribution of its gifted General Manager, Sir Herbert Walker. But the general economic depression did not create a climate

Then: Undated, c1937
New products need to be promoted; this Southern Railway van was advertising the 'Portsmouth Direct' electrification. Complete with a representation of a 4COR unit and a four aspect colour light signal(!), the display is thought to be at Portsmouth Harbour. *Author's Collection*

Now: 30 August 1998
This tile of 55 Broadway is one of several designs which graced London Underground stations in the late 1930s. This version is at St John's Wood station, which opened in 1939. *Author*

in which the undertakings prospered.

A new era began in 1933 with the creation of the London Passenger Transport Board. The Board had a general duty 'to secure the provision of an adequate and properly co-ordinated system of passenger transport...', to meet the needs of London.

Main Line Traffics

Despite the efforts of the other companies in the interwar period, the laurels must surely go to the London & North Eastern Railway with its extensive fleet of Pacifics built under the direction of Sir Nigel Gresley. The railway introduced the 'Silver Jubilee', the 'West Riding' and the 'Coronation', all of which were streamlined expresses from King's Cross in the late

1930s. Churchward and Collett, Maunsell and Bulleid, and Stanier, are all names associated with the advance of locomotive design. But it was the LNER, with its superbly engineered East Coast main line which allowed it to make the most of the power available. In 1938, this secured for the company the world speed record for steam traction.

With freight, the picture was less encouraging. The same period saw the launch of the 'Square Deal' campaign, in which the main line railways sought to reduce the advantageous competitive position of the road freight industry. Effectively, no progress was made, and the outbreak of war secured the position of the railways in the nation's transport requirements for the duration.

Electrification

Besides the Southern, other railways electrified by the outbreak of World War 2 were the Euston-Watford local and the North London Broad Street-Richmond lines of the LMS, and their branches. These had fourth rail dc traction supplies, as opposed to the third rail of the Southern.

All of this activity took place against the background of an expanding population, which had a continuing tendency to live further and further from the centre of London. 'Live in Metro-land' was a deliberate ploy by the Metropolitan Railway Company, but the suburban expansion was made possible by the railways and the Underground together. Later, Green Belt planning policies limited the extent of further expansion; as a result, some parts of London Transport's New Works Programme of 1935-40 were never executed. The outstanding Central Line works were completed in 1949. However, the proposed Northern Line extensions from Moorgate via Finsbury Park to Alexandra Palace and to East Finchley, and from Mill Hill East to Edgware and then Bushey Heath were at first postponed and subsequently abandoned altogether. On the Southern, work on extending the Chessington branch of 1938 to Leatherhead was never resumed after the end of hostilities. No new houses meant no potential traffic for the railway.

World War 2 put much strain on an already run-down system, to say nothing of the damage inflicted by the war itself. Nationalisation in 1948 was not accompanied by funds to rebuild the railways, other than to complete some of the half finished business under way at the outbreak of hostilities. The outstanding main line scheme was the Liverpool Street-Shenfield electrification, completed in 1949 with the then favoured 1,500V dc overhead. Chelmsford and Southend Victoria were added to the electrified network in 1956. The electrification of the Metropolitan beyond Rickmansworth did not materialise until 1960. This latter also signalled the end of the electric locomotive and steam working for passenger services on London Underground.

Then: 27 September 1935
The 'Silver Jubilee', a super streamlined train makes its final test run from King's Cross to Peterborough and back, eight days before it was introduced into commercial service. The 'Silver Jubilee' ran to Newcastle upon Tyne at an average 70.3mph, giving an end to end journey time comfortably less than four hours. It is seen here leaving King's Cross behind LNER 'A4' Pacific No 2509 *Silver Link*. *Author's Collection*

Then: 31 July 1943
Paddington's platforms are undeniably busy, and trains will be very full. The date is a Saturday in the middle of the war, but it is also the August Bank Holiday weekend. Motorway tailbacks were not a concern of those times.
Ian Allan Library

Then: 2 October 1940
Enemy destruction of railway facilities was of varying severity. This was the Stonebridge Park electric carriage sheds of the LMS. *Author's Collection*

Then, and very soon after: 27 December 1940
This remarkable pair of pictures, thanks to the censor, is of a location identified only as being 'in the Eastern suburbs'. Six-track formations are however uncommon, and it seems most likely to be somewhere on the Liverpool Street side of Stratford. They show the results of bomb damage and the same scene a few hours later on the same day. Use of labour was prodigious, and at least 60 men are visible in the earlier picture. *Author's Collection* (2)

Postwar Recovery

The whole approach seemed geared to returning matters to where they stood in 1939, with little acknowledgement that times had moved on. The day of the steam engine was, in effect, over. Nowhere was this more apparent than in the expansion of road competition, whether by haulier or private car. It was not until 1955 that the Modernisation Plan for British Railways was launched. This, a full decade after the end of hostilities, speaks volumes for the government of the day's priority for the transport industries.

But the £1.2 billion plan (contemporary prices) did seem a trifle lacking in vision. For instance, it laid great emphasis on the reorganisation of freight traffic and the construction of large scale marshalling yards. With the benefit of hindsight, these appear to have been capital intensive projects, using vast areas of land, in which an oversized wagon fleet was parked for an extended period during which it earned no revenue. The subsequent history of freight carryings by rail tends to confirm this rather cynical view; this was a situation retrieved to some extent by the later development of the block or unit train which needed no such facilities. Trainload operation, whether of coal, metals, construction or petroleum products, or in containers or as automotive products, was to prove a far more productive venture.

More positively, the Modernisation Plan presaged a complete elimination of steam traction, to be replaced with diesel or electric traction. It is a salutary reminder of the scale of the supporting infrastructure to recall that even the Southern Region, already with substantial electric services, had steam sheds at Nine Elms, Feltham, Guildford, Stewarts Lane, Bricklayers Arms, Hither Green, Tonbridge, Redhill, Norwood Junction, Horsham, Three Bridges and Tunbridge Wells West in the area under review, as late as 1959. A similar pattern could be seen elsewhere.

Fleets of diesel locomotives and diesel multiple-units were procured, and established themselves with varying degrees of success. It was believed widely that, where electrification was the ultimate aim, the intermediate stage of dieselisation should have been eliminated. The mixing of new diesel engines with the coal dust, soot and clinker of a steam motive power depot was unlikely to achieve the best results for the new traction.

The Bournemouth electrification, commissioned in 1967, represented the final fling of steam traction in the London area. Steam locomotives, still being constructed as late as 1960, were eliminated from standard gauge tracks by British Railways nationally in 1968.

One objective of electrification was to increase commuter carrying capacity. The 1949 experiments with double-deck

London Railway Developement

Then: 27 January 1959
The large modern hump marshalling yard at Temple Mills, Stratford, has now been abandoned. This was the view from the Control Tower, showing the secondary retarders for one of the fans of sidings. Retarders were used by the Control Tower staff to apply pressure in varying degrees to the wheel flanges to slow the descending wagons. The aim was to make sure that the wagon had enough momentum to reach any other wagons in the siding, but not to slam into them, while at the same time allowing for the rollability of each wagon and the effect of weather conditions on the rail surfaces.
Author's Collection

Then: Undated, *c*1955
Although the Modernisation Plan diesel locomotives were purchased by the British Transport Commission from a variety of manufacturers, the 3,300hp *Deltic* locomotive was a private venture by the English Electric Co. After running experimentally, notably on the London Midland Region, the eventual outcome was the purchase of 22 machines for the East Coast main line and the consignment of the prototype to the Science Museum. English Electric doubtless hoped for more sales, but the production versions acquitted themselves well and a lot better than some of the other BTC acquisitions. The prototype weighed in at 106 tons, a relative lightweight.
Author's Collection

electric trains on the South Eastern lines to Dartford were judged unsuccessful, partly because station dwell times increased due to the slowness of passenger access, but also because of ventilation problems. This resulted in the alternative approach, which was a decision to lengthen platforms to take 10 rather than eight cars.

The coaching fleets of British Railways were almost entirely renewed, whether as locomotive-hauled or multiple-unit vehicles. Certainly, the railway industry itself has moved on over the years; one of the most recent developments seems to be a move back from three-plus-two seating to two-plus-two seats (each side of the gangway). Seating may be more comfortable, but there is by definition less of it. London Underground has also reduced seating.

AC Electrics

Most of the Great Eastern suburban services of British Railways were electrified at 25kV ac in 1960 as the Chenford (Chingford, Enfield, Hertford East — via the reopened route through Southbury — and Bishop's Stortford) scheme. The London, Tilbury & Southend line was completed in 1961, and beyond Chelmsford to Colchester in 1963. The whole included the conversion of the then dc lines to ac. Some sections (including Fenchurch Street to Barking) were at one time 6.25kV ac, but all became 25kV ac in the late 1970s or early 1980s.

The missing Lea Valley link was added in 1969 and Witham-

Braintree in 1977. Other London area work has wired the line between Stratford and Tottenham Hale/Seven Sisters, Romford and Upminster, and the new link to Stansted Airport.

The Southern's electrification, already so well established, was extended to the Kent coast in 1959/61 and Bournemouth in 1967. Other infilling schemes have resulted in the whole of that company's passenger network within 30 miles of the centre of London being operated by electric trains, other than the Oxted-Uckfield and Reading-Redhill services.

The term InterCity was the product name bestowed on the electric expresses which provided the London Midland Region services between Euston and Manchester and Euston and Liverpool from 1966. In that context, it combined speed and frequency of service with a higher quality of train. Conceptually, InterCity was a long way from the occasional 'crack express' teamed with a number of other services of less than outstanding performance, which had been the norm up until then.

Electrification of the West Coast main line also saw ac outer suburban services become operational. Further electrification has seen much of the North London line equipped for ac, for the benefit primarily of freight traffic to and from the Great Eastern main line. Electrification also followed the reintroduction of passenger services between Dalston and Stratford, partially in compensation for the loss of services to Broad Street. With the later decommissioning of the third rail on some stretches and its replacement with 25kV overhead, what are now the North Woolwich-Richmond services require dual system units for their operation.

Then: 1 July 1966
The end of steam at Waterloo sees
Standard Class 5 4-6-0 No 73087
Linette waiting to depart with a train
for Salisbury, while station pilot
Standard Class 3 2-6-2T No 82029
runs light to the yard. *B. H. Jackson*

Then: 14 September 1949
The pair of 4DD double-deck trains were introduced
experimentally on the Cannon Street-Dartford routes on
2 November 1949. An eight-car train had a total seating capacity
of 1,104, but this did include 88 tip-up seats. The comparison
was with a 2x4EPB formation with 772 seats, or a 43% gain.
This is unit 4001, photographed before the two trains entered
service. *Author's Collection*

The Great Northern had to wait rather longer. 1976 saw
electrification of the inner suburban services, Moorgate to
Welwyn Garden City/Hertford North. This incorporated most of
the GN&C line between Finsbury Park and Moorgate, opened
as an electric railway in 1904. The tunnel section is third rail
dc, with changeover to overhead ac at Drayton Park.
Electrification was extended in 1978/79 to the GN outer
suburban services, including King's Cross itself and beyond to
Hitchin and (initially) Royston. The rest of the East Coast main
line followed, with Peterborough reached in 1987.

The Midland line was also electrified, as far as Bedford, and at
the London end to St Pancras and to Moorgate, Widened Lines.
Services commenced in 1983, but in 1988 Thameslink services
were commissioned. Their operation included the rehabilitation
of the Snow Hill tunnel from Blackfriars and the building of an
underground City Thameslink station. This replaced Holborn
Viaduct. Third rail electrification was carried out, with voltage
changeover at Farringdon.

The most recent large scale scheme has been the
electrification of the Great Western main line to a point west of
Hayes & Harlington, and the new BAA branch to Heathrow
Airport. This does not affect the local services, which remain
diesel unit operated, as do those from Marylebone.

Frequently, electrification has been accompanied by
resignalling, both because of track realignments and new
layouts making work necessary, but also to capitalise on the
capacity benefits which electrification could bring. In any case,
much of the semaphore equipment was worn out.

Then: 8 June 1957
Carriage interiors in the postwar era were strictly functional.
This 3+2 seating layout was typical, representing what was
described as the London District Three-Car sets of BR Standard
Design of 1957 for the LMR. These SR Eastleigh-built units, later
known as Class 501, differed from domestic production only by
their short 57ft underframes as opposed to the standard
63ft 6in. *Author's Collection*

Now: 8 November 1997
Recent production includes the Class 365 dual voltage units for both WAGN and Connex SouthEastern. The interior is more spacious, with 2+2 seating and sliding doors. Some seats are 'face to back' as opposed to facing pairs. This is a WAGN unit. *Author*

Now: 11 April 1998
London Underground's 1996 stock for the Jubilee Line has four spaces set aside in each car for the use of mothers with pushchairs or those in wheelchairs. All seating is longitudinal, with the net effect of only 34 seats being provided per car. The 1983 stock, which it replaced, had 48 seats. *Author*

This led to the introduction of power signalling schemes, controlled from specially constructed signalboxes covering often large areas and with panels which can set up entire routes with the minimum of switching. More recent schemes as at Marylebone and at Liverpool Street have moved on again, to Integrated Electronic Control Centre (IECC) schemes. Marylebone takes the whole of the remaining GC operation and the Joint route to beyond Bicester, excluding the section owned by London Underground between Harrow and Amersham. The Liverpool Street IECC exerts control of the Great Eastern main line for nearly 50 miles, to the far side of Marks Tey as well as the branches to Southend Central and to Southminster. There is also provision for some bi-directional working if required.

The net effect is that the semaphore signal is now a decided rarity, as some of the photographs show. The colour light with no moving parts and high visibility in darkness and in fog has now achieved a convincing dominance.

Major civil engineering schemes have been the construction of Waterloo International station, North Pole depot for servicing Eurostar trains, and the Nine Elms flyover to allow the trains to access the Chatham lines out of Victoria.

Railway Closures

Less encouragingly, there have been some line closures. Mostly these have affected the more rural parts of the area under consideration. Others are associated with major investment

Then: 2 March 1958
Preparation for electrification is underway at Timberlog Lane between Basildon and Pitsea on the London, Tilbury & Southend line. The track is being upgraded and the final covering of ballast is being spread to carry the track. The locomotive is not identified. *Author's Collection*

London Railway Developement

Then: 26 January 1982
The closure of the by then underused Broad Street was part of the price to be paid for the Broadgate office development. This view was taken from the NatWest tower and shows a Class 501 unit arriving; the spare land around is all too obvious. By then, Broad Street was dealing with a mere 4,500 commuters a day. *Martin Bond*

Then: 1 October 1959
A Class 08 shunter is being used on what was described as pre-electrification work at Palmers Green on the Hertford North branch. Sheet steel piling is being driven at the bottom of embankments, to stabilise them. The Great Northern suburban electrification eventually went live on 8 November 1976. *Author's Collection*

Then: 19 January 1984
This was the view from a little north of Blackfriars station, looking straight ahead to the Holborn Viaduct terminus, and below left to the Snow Hill tunnel and the route through to the Widened Lines at Farringdon. *Ian Allan Library*

schemes, such as Croydon Tramlink. Although closures are identified particularly with the name of Dr (later Lord) Beeching and his 1963 report 'The Reshaping of British Railways', many of the service withdrawals in the southeast took place rather earlier. Post-1948, line closures have included the following. This list is not exhaustive.

• On the Great Eastern, the Seven Sisters-Palace Gates branch, Angel Road to Lower Edmonton, Bishop's Stortford-Braintree & Bocking, the Buntingford branch from St Margarets, and all railways to Maldon. Extending the Central Line east of Stratford saw the end of the Seven Kings to Newbury Park link. Services from Tottenham Hale to Stratford have been discontinued and connections to the Chingford branch removed, while the Graham Road curve between the North London and Great Eastern lines in the Hackney area both opened and closed.

• On the Great Northern, the Finsbury Park-Alexandra Palace branch, the cross-country routes linking Hertford to Welwyn Garden City, Luton and Dunstable, also Hatfield to St Albans, and the curves from Finsbury Park to Canonbury and King's Cross (York Way) to Farringdon.

• On the Midland, the line from Harpenden to Hemel Hempstead, and the curve from Kentish Town to Upper Holloway. On the London & North Western, the branch from Harrow & Wealdstone to Stanmore and the line from Dalston Junction to Broad Street.

• On the Great Western, the two branches from West Drayton to Staines West and to Uxbridge Vine Street, from Denham to Uxbridge High Street (GW/GC Joint), and the line between Bourne End and High Wycombe. Also, the branches from Princes Risborough to Watlington and to Thame and Oxford.

• On the London & South Western, the line from Brookwood to Bisley Camp, the curve from Frimley to the South Western main line, and the Tongham loop avoiding Aldershot.

• On the Brighton, closures include all the lines radiating from East Grinstead except that to London, Tunbridge Wells Central to Eridge, the electrified Haywards Heath to Horsted Keynes branch, and Guildford to Horsham.

• On the South Eastern, the rural branch from Dunton Green to Westerham has long gone. The lines between Woodside and Sanderstead, and from Elmers End to Addiscombe have also been closed, but parts of these and also the Wimbledon-West Croydon line are being reused for Croydon Tramlink. The withdrawal of the Nunhead to Crystal Palace High Level service took place as long ago as 1954.

Sad though the closures may have been, none of these lines could be claimed to be essential to the fabric of a healthy railway system. Network stability in the London area, in comparison with elsewhere in the country, was the order of the day.
It should also be said that some lines threatened by Beeching remain today. These include:

• Watford Junction-St Albans Abbey
• Romford-Upminster
• Witham-Braintree & Bocking
• Clapham Junction-Kensington (Olympia)

All of these have since been electrified, as has the Redhill-Tonbridge section of the Reading-Tonbridge line, on which local services were also listed for withdrawal. Indeed, the Kensington (Olympia) electric services now continue north to Willesden Junction.
There have been negligible closures of individual stations. Into this category come the assortment of Coulsdon North, East Brixton, Low Street, Primrose Hill and Tilbury Riverside. A few have been closed temporarily from time to time on safety grounds or for reasons of vandalism or arson.

Now: 11 November 1998
From the Blackfriars station platform, Thameslink trains are seen (left) disappearing towards City Thameslink and (right) breasting the climb to Blackfriars. These are both dual voltage Class 319 units; a third rail only unit cannot proceed further north than Farringdon. *Author*

Now: 2 April 1998
Waterloo International was built on the site use previously by the Windsor line platforms. This view is of the low level concourse. *Author*

The Underground has had very few service withdrawals, particularly if one discounts the Amersham to Aylesbury operations now provided by Chiltern Railways. The Acton Town to South Acton branch ceased operation in 1959, and the Epping to Ongar and Holborn to Aldwych branches in 1994. However, LUL is not averse to extended temporary closures 'for essential engineering work'. Mornington Crescent station and the whole of the East London Line were both closed in recent times for a matter of several years.

Commuter Travel

Where do commuters using National Railways arrive in London? Overwhelmingly, the stations serving the suburbs and towns to the south and east of London carry the majority. This

Then: 5 June 1937
The Alexandra Palace branch from Finsbury Park was closed permanently on 5 July 1954, having already suffered periods of closure due to shortages of fuel. This view shows the north side of the Palace, with Class N2 0-6-2T No 4587 awaiting departure for King's Cross. *H. C. Casserley*

Now: 15 October 1998
The area once used for the station platforms is now a car park for exhibitors, but the station building, centre left, is an old-people's day centre. It is unmistakably Great Northern. There was a direct entrance to the Palace from the platforms, the bridge portion of which still exists and is just visible in the photograph. *Author*

is one effect of the relative lack of Underground services south of the river, but also the extent to which the main line companies saw it in their interests to pursue commuter traffic in the past. Those who had other traffic objectives, principally those serving north and west London and the area in between, were more inclined to let the Underground develop the local traffic and reap any benefits.

An analysis of the morning peak arrivals, defined as 07.00-09.59, showed the following in 1993.

• Fenchurch Street	24,200	6%
• Liverpool Street	57,600	15%
• King's Cross/St Pancras	19,900	5%
• Euston	15,700	4%
• Marylebone	5,600	2%
• Paddington	12,800	3%
• Victoria	51,300	13%
• Waterloo	55,600	15%
• London Bridge	42,200	11%
• Charing Cross	36,400	10%
• Cannon Street	27,700	7%
• Blackfriars	10,300	3%
• others	22,700	6%
Total	382,000	100%

Passenger volumes have increased since 1993 by about 15%, but the general picture and the proportions of travellers are unlikely to have changed much.

Waterloo and Liverpool Street are the busiest points of arrival in the morning peak. Half of all arrivals at main line stations make an onward leg of their journey to their final destination by foot. They tend to be concentrated at termini within or near the City of London, such as Cannon Street or London Bridge. The 38% who use the Underground for their onward journey are drawn more heavily from those stations further away from employment areas, such as Euston, Paddington and King's Cross. The station with the biggest proportion of bus users is Victoria at 18%, reflecting perhaps the bus station in the forecourt, while the lowest proportion who walk to their final destination are those arriving at Paddington at 16%.

New Railway Construction

Considering the changes to London's railways over the last half century, the railway network has been remarkably stable in terms of its extent. Of the new traffic sources which have been tapped, airports are probably the most important:

ROWFANT

Then: undated, *c*1965
The Three Bridges-East Grinstead service was closed on 2 January 1967 and Rowfant station is seen here with auto-trains crossing. This view was taken looking west towards Three Bridges. *G. S. Robinson*

Now: 23 September 1998
The boarded up main station building is all that remains in this view, located just within the boundaries of what is now an industrial site. *Author*

BLAKE HALL

Then: 1 March 1977
The likelihood of being able to photograph a London Underground train in service, with little else but open fields in view, has been diminished by the closure of the 9.85km Epping-Ongar branch of the Central Line on 1 October 1994. Here, a 1962 stock train leaves Blake Hall for Epping, deep in the Essex countryside. The line has now been sold to Pilot Developments, who intend to restart services. *Author*

ALDWYCH

Then: 28 September 1994
The 0.6km Holborn-Aldwych service was withdrawn finally on 1 October 1994, its end precipitated by the urgent need to replace the Aldwych lifts. These dated from the line's opening in 1907, and usage was said not to justify the expense. In reality, the line itself was something of an anomaly, caused by the amalgamation of Underground interests through which the present Piccadilly Line was created, but not until after the construction of what became the branch. This photograph shows 1973 stock at the Aldwych terminus, shortly before closure. *Author*

HEATHROW TERMINAL 4

Now: 27 May 1998
The Heathrow Express service commenced public operations on 25 May 1998. This photograph shows unit No 332012 preparing to depart from Terminal 4. At this stage, the fourth cars had not been marshalled into the trains. *Author*

• Gatwick Airport. The former Gatwick Racecourse station on the Brighton line, built in 1891 but rarely used since the outbreak of World War 2, was rebuilt, resignalled and renamed Gatwick Airport on 28 May 1958. Shortly afterwards, the airport itself was commissioned. This was a rare example of the railway being in place right from the start.

• Heathrow Airport. After years of vacillation, it was finally decided to extend the Piccadilly Line of London Underground from Hounslow West to Hatton Cross and Heathrow Central (later, Heathrow Terminals 1,2,3). This opened in 1975/77, but the decision not to build Terminal 4 where intended originally resulted in the construction of a loop arrangement, opened in 1986. This was followed by the BAAline from Paddington, in 1998.

• Stansted Airport. The third London Airport was opened in 1991, served by a new branch from the GE Cambridge line. Journey time is 41 or 42 minutes for the 37.50 miles from Liverpool Street.

• London City Airport. The long-established Silvertown station on the line to North Woolwich has been branded 'for London

STANSTED AIRPORT

Now: 15 April 1991.
Stansted Airport is a modern twin-platform station with a centre bay at the outer end. This latter is designed to hold short two-car diesel units, keeping their exhaust fumes out of the airport station proper. In this view, No 322485, one of the four units then dedicated to Stansted Express work, departs with the 16.30 to Liverpool Street.
Author

City Airport', but the only means of reaching the latter is by a dreary quarter-mile walk through the streets. It is now planned to serve the airport with the Docklands Light Railway.

• Luton Airport Parkway station opened in 1999. The station is served by Thameslink, and a dedicated bus service is provided to and from the airport terminal.

Other major new construction works have been on London Underground, with the opening of the Victoria line (1968-72), Jubilee Line Baker Street to Charing Cross (1979), and the Jubilee Line Extension from Green Park to Stratford (1999).

In a different category is the Princess Royal Distribution Terminal for the Post Office at Willesden, the biggest railway station to be built in Britain in the 20th century. This seven-platformed building is now the centre for all railway mail work, and a fleet of 16 electric multiple-unit trains has been purpose-built for work nationally. These are supplemented by locomotive-hauled services, especially on non-electrified parts of the system.

Of all the investment schemes, that for the West Coast main line promises a major upgrading of both infrastructure and service provision. The proposed introduction of the Advanced Passenger Train (APT) never progressed beyond the experimental stage; progress now is a matter for the franchisee Virgin Trains and Railtrack between them.

There are also the frustrated schemes. Perhaps the most ambitious one which nearly but did not quite leave the drawing board is CrossRail. The plan is to provide the benefits of a new cross-London underground link for full-sized trains, between Shenfield in the east and both Reading and Aylesbury in the west. Trains would take the present line as far as the Bethnal Green area, then run underground to stations at Liverpool Street, Farringdon, Tottenham Court Road, Bond Street and Paddington. They would rise to the surface and join the present railway to Reading, while trains for Aylesbury would take the Dudding Hill freight-only line to join the Great Central at Neasden. Services in the east could start from as far afield as Southend Central, while in the west the expanding Heathrow Airport must be a contender as a destination if capacity is available.

Naturally, trains would be electric. While the Great Eastern and now the Great Western as far as Airport Junction are both electrified at 25kV ac, the Metropolitan is of course fourth rail

WILLESDEN

Now: 23 September 1997
The Princess Royal Distribution Terminal sees No 325002 and a PCV (Propelling Control Vehicle) in the terminal. The PCVs, former Class 307 Driving Trailers, are used for low speed manoeuvres to allow locomotive-hauled trains to be reversed for short distances in the Willesden area, before the locomotive heads the train in the normal manner. They do not have the full facilities of a Driving Van Trailer, and the locomotive may be either diesel or electric. *Author*

CHEDDINGTON

Then: August 1983
The great white hope of the 1970s and early 1980s, an Advanced Passenger Train formation speeds south through Cheddington towards Euston. The tilting concept features again in the trains to be supplied for the West Coast main line for Virgin Trains, and it is to be hoped fervently that they meet with more success than did the APT. *Author*

PADDINGTON

Then and now: 11 April 1998
What was once a railway-owned hotel is now in private ownership. This is the Great Western Royal in Praed Street, Paddington, with the GWR monogram still very plain for all to see. *Author*

CLAPHAM JUNCTION

Then and now: 2 September 1998
Nobody could be unsure of the owners or function of this property in St John's Hill, Clapham Junction, though unfortunately for anybody wishing to send a parcel, the doors are firmly closed. *Author*

dc. The choice is either dual electrification systems on the Metropolitan section, or two changes of traction current during the journey at both Neasden and Amersham.

Such a scheme allows passengers to travel without a change to a number of central London destinations, but it also frees platform capacity at the existing London terminals for other uses.

In the meantime, the Thameslink 2000 scheme will, it is hoped, provide similar benefits on a north-south axis across London.

Finally, light rail schemes. The first stage of the Docklands Light Railway opened from Tower Gateway and Stratford to Island Gardens in 1987, with subsequent extensions. Croydon Tramlink is also under construction, with services to run from Wimbledon to Croydon and Addiscombe, and northern routes to Elmers End and Beckenham Junction.

A total of 18 new stations have been opened on existing lines since 1960, and these are listed in Appendix II.

A major innovation has been the establishment of the Eurostar services from Waterloo International through the Channel Tunnel to Paris and to Brussels. It is intended that these will at some time in the future be rerouted via the Channel Tunnel Rail Link to St Pancras.

Yet, beside all the new developments, some features have remained remarkably static. The railway itself is slow to change. Where in London can one today find a Great Western symbol from the pre-1948 company, still proudly displayed, or a building bearing the name of a pre-Grouping company? The pictures here provide the answer, but it is not suggested that these are the only examples.

In the descriptions which follow, the timetable used for analysis purposes is the 1998/99 winter timetable, and the section headings refer to the pre-1923 railway companies. Service frequencies quoted refer generally to the midday off-peak services on Mondays to Fridays.

London, Tilbury & Southend

Fenchurch Street counts among the earlier of London's railway terminals, although the present building dates mainly from 1853. The four-platformed station, with its two-track main line approach, has a busy line occupation; 20 trains arrive in the heaviest morning peak hour on Mondays to Fridays. Platform lengths are such that these may be 12-car trains.

This latter-day appendage of the Midland Railway has a catchment limited by the Thames on the south side and the Great Eastern line to the north. While the main line to Shoeburyness operates via Upminster and Basildon (4tph basic off-peak frequency), there are two other routes. Using the extensive flyovers west of Barking, some trains run via Dagenham Dock to terminate at Grays (2tph). Other services continue to Upminster and reach Grays via Ockendon and Chafford Hundred. These then continue via Tilbury to Pitsea and Southend Central (also 2tph).

The Docklands Light Railway terminates alongside the Fenchurch Street station throat, and occupies two of the tracks formerly available to the LTS from the terminus to Stepney East (now Limehouse). Where the DLR continues towards Poplar, the LTS swings to the north; there is a single-track electrified link towards Stratford, which has never gained a regular passenger service.

There is a strong Underground presence in the form of the District Line, which runs alongside the main line from Campbell Road Junction (no longer any more than a converging point) and Upminster. The Underground trains serve all the intermediate stations, whereas LTS Rail's services have for many years called only at Barking. Hammersmith & City Line services of LUL do not run further east than Barking.

A variation in the service provision occurs after 22.00, when Fenchurch Street, itself without any direct Underground connection, closes. Services are then diverted to Liverpool Street via Forest Gate Junction, and call also at Stratford. All trains are operated by the franchisee LTS Rail.

A new station has been constructed at West Ham for LTS Rail. This provides direct interchange with the Jubilee Line and the North London line, as well as the District and Hammersmith & City Lines. LTS passengers for Canary Wharf find that the Jubilee Line offers a much more direct route than those available previously, and it should not be overlooked that the presence of the Jubilee Line provides a connection to the West End with only one change. The tiresome walk from Fenchurch Street to the Central line at Bank thus becomes unnecessary.

There is substantial freight traffic associated with the extensive industrial and port facilities on north Thameside.

All lines are now electrified at 25kV ac, some parts previously at 6.25kV ac.

FENCHURCH STREET

Then: 20 May 1980
Fenchurch Street station sits tightly surrounded by office buildings at the concourse end, though this changes rapidly at the 'country' end of the station. In this view along Platforms 1 and 2, a pair of Class 302 units, Nos 302238 and 302255, await departure. These trains virtually monopolised the service provision for 30 years.

Now: 28 October 1998
With a viewpoint a little further distant, the most obvious change is in the commercial buildings in the background. Yellow lines have appeared on the platforms, and No 310084 is departing from Platform 3. *Author (2)*

STEPNEY EAST/ LIMEHOUSE

Then: 27 September 1983
No 302263 leads a train towards Fenchurch Street round the tight curve through a station which is still traditional in its fittings. Located on arches above ground level, the wooden-boarded platforms are of note.

Now: 28 October 1998
The front end of No 310070 appears almost as a cardboard cut out, confirming that it is a four-car train only. Changes at this station, which is now an interchange for the Docklands Light Railway, are minimal; those wanting the DLR have to descend first to street level. The up side canopies have been cut back, and the station renamed. *Author (2)*

BARKING

Then: 1 March 1981
The massive construction of flyovers in the late 1950s preceded electrification of the London, Tilbury & Southend. The objective was to eliminate conflicting movements between British Railways and the Underground, and to allow the BR trains to proceed unhindered in either of the directions available, both east and west. A ballast train with No 37259 in charge begins the haul up onto the westbound flyover which will take it to the Tottenham & Hampstead line, while a District Line train of D stock is also beginning its climb on a route which will take it to the north side of the LT&S but beneath the T&H route.

Now: 28 October 1998
From a viewpoint on the next bridge to the east, a District Line train leaves Platform 6 for Richmond. The Tilbury line platforms are on the right. There has been little change in the area generally, but a new footbridge is under construction on the left side of the picture.
Les Bertram/Author

UPMINSTER

Then: 20 May 1980
This is a large seven-platform station, though only two platforms are used for the through LT&S services. Here, Class 302 unit No 244 arrives with a down service for Pitsea.

Now: 7 November 1998
From the same footbridge, the view here includes No 317329 (to Fenchurch Street), No 10089 (to Southend Central) and two LUL District Line trains of D stock. A small passenger shelter has appeared, as has new lighting. *Author (2)*

PITSEA

Then: 20 May 1980
Class 302 unit No 302281 is in the main line Platform 2 before running via Upminster to Fenchurch Street. The nuisance value of slam door stock is evident. If passengers themselves don't shut the doors after use, who will?

BASILDON

Then: November 1974

The then Eastern Region was very reluctant to construct a new station to serve Basildon, arguing that Laindon at rather more than one mile away or Pitsea at two miles were quite adequate. Finance came, eventually, from the local authority. In the 1991 passenger counts, Basildon totals comfortably outstripped the two other stations combined.

Now: 7 November 1998

Little has changed on the station itself, although there is much more commercial development in the vicinity. A Class 310 unit leaves in the down direction.
Ian Allan Library/Author

Now: 28 October 1998

No 312795 draws to a halt in the almost identical position. There is little apparent change, even with the television screens for passenger information. Somewhat disconcertingly for passengers, the other footbridge does not give access to the line to Stanford-le-Hope and Tilbury (out of the picture on the extreme right). That has to be reached using the bridge on which the photographer is standing.
Author (2)

LEIGH-ON-SEA

Then: 20 May 1980
This picture certainly has a period feel about it, with No 302279 approaching on the down line and bound for Shoeburyness. The signalbox controlled the by then obsolete design searchlight-style signal for trains starting from the central bay platform.

28 October 1998
Two decades later, all signalling control is under Upminster, and bi-directional signalling is in force as evidenced by the choice of routes offered by the starting signal. The track layout is unchanged, including the sand drag used to trap any train should the starting signal be disobeyed. *Author (2)*

SOUTHEND CENTRAL

Then: 7 August 1961
Steam operation is in its final throes as Stanier 2-6-4T No 42528 prepares to leave with the 14.00 to Fenchurch Street. This is at least a 10-coach train. Overhead electrification is already in place.

WESTCLIFF

Then: 1 September 1963
The attractions of Southend have brought day-trippers over the years in trainloads. Here, Class 27 No D5397 is at the head of a train of non-corridor BR suburban stock, forming the 09.40 Luton to Southend Central as it approached Westcliff. The journey time is unlikely to have been much less than 2hr.

Now: 6 November 1998
The cascade of Class 317 units from West Anglia services is exemplified here by No 317305 on a service from Fenchurch Street via Tilbury. Originally for the Midland Suburban Electrics, these trains are distinguishable by their opening but unglazed hopper ventilators. *Peter Ashton (2)*

Now: 4 November 1998
No 312727 is the present motive power in a little changed scene. This is one of the trains which were not equipped for working on 6.25kV ac, but this is nowadays of no consequence. *Peter Ashton (2)*

DAGENHAM DOCK

Then: 9 February 1978
The up line on this snowy morning sees Class 302 No 301 arriving with a Fenchurch Street service. The Class 08 in the background is the shunter for the Ford works.

Now: 28 October 1998
From a higher viewpoint on the footbridge, Class 90 No 90143 *Freightliner Coatbridge* speeds over the level crossing with a train from Tilbury. The signalbox, now demolished, has been replaced by the Upminster installation. *Author (2)*

GRAYS

Then: November 1980
The Class 302 units were very ordinary, but they did their work. No 273 is arriving at Grays with an up service, over a level crossing which is no more than a foot crossing. Even then, it has sufficient usage to justify the provision of a bridge when the crossing is closed.

GRAYS

Then: 1 March 1977
The 112 Class 302 units did not monopolise the Fenchurch Street services, since there were a total of nine in which a full length luggage van replaced passenger accommodation. This was to cater for the long departed Tilbury boat train traffic which ran traditionally to and from St Pancras. Class 308/2 No 320 arrives from Fenchurch Street at Grays in decidedly unpleasant conditions.

Now: 28 October 1998
The down side shelter has been replaced. It houses the ticket barriers which at that time were yet to be commissioned. A Class 317 unit is approaching with what are presently operated as services to Southend Central via Ockendon. *Author (2)*

Now: 28 October 1998
Resignalling has meant the abolition of the signalbox. No 310075 approaches in a scene which has otherwise changed little. *Author (2)*

TILBURY RIVERSIDE

Then: 26 September 1979
This was a large imposing terminus, which of course meant that trains had to reverse if using it as an intermediate station. Here, it shows all the signs of a typical such station, goods yard on the left. In the platforms are Class 302 unit No 306 and Class 308/2 unit No 317.

Now: 28 October 1998
Closure of Tilbury Riverside station in 1993 and its replacement by a bus service from Tilbury Town allowed the station site to be redeveloped for rail freight. While the buildings in the background remain unscathed, it must be said that freight is noticeable by its absence. These views are both taken from the nearest available access road.

Now: 28 October 1998
Underneath the bridge carrying the access road was to be found No 08764, a 350hp shunter in a delicate shade of pale blue and parked thus presumably to keep it out of the rain. *Author (3)*

OCKENDON

Then: 6 September 1958
Heavy rain the previous night brought flooding to Ockendon and a discussion between staff outside the signalbox on the then down platform. At this stage, the Metro-Cammell Class 101 unit would have been almost brand-new, and its ability to cope with such conditions somewhat uncertain.

Now: 7 November 1998
Today, the signalbox and semaphores have gone, and the up platform is not in normal use. No 310089 is leaving the station with a train for Southend Central. The scaffolding on the station building was a result of repair work and not demolition.
Frank Church/Author

The Great Eastern

Liverpool Street is a relative newcomer to the ranks of London termini, not having opened until 1875 and then as a mere 10-platformed station. Until this time, passengers had to detrain in the unsalubrious and relatively remote area of Shoreditch. So successful was the new station that, coupled with the cheap workmen's fares which the Great Eastern Railway was obliged to offer, passenger volumes were such that the station was expanded to 18 platforms less than 20 years later. This was the new east side, separated from the west side by the extended lengths of Platforms 9 and 10. These were used for the Norwich services and the Harwich boat trains, respectively.

Since then, Liverpool Street has been entirely reconstructed. The work was completed in 1991/92 as part of the Broadgate office development. Among the benefits to passengers is the extensive concourse area extending across the ends of all platforms, which now have a uniform barrier line.

From Liverpool Street, six lines proceed in parallel as far as Bethnal Green, where the northernmost pair diverge to form a four-track section to Hackney Downs. Here they split, those on the west side continuing to the Enfield Town terminus, or via the Southbury loop to Cheshunt. Those on the east side run via Hackney Downs and Clapton tunnels to Clapton Junction, dividing again to reach Chingford or Tottenham Hale and the Lea Valley main line. This latter proceeds via Cheshunt to Broxbourne, where a branch to Hertford East diverges, and

LIVERPOOL STREET

Then: 5 August 1961
A view from the cab road sees 'Britannia' Pacific No 70011 *Hotspur*, a Norwich engine, ready to depart from Liverpool Street's Platform 11 with the 18.33 commuter service to Clacton. Behind it is an unidentified Class 37 locomotive. The steam age in East Anglia was nearly over, and both platforms are wired for electric traction.

Now: 24 September 1998
It is possible to obtain glimpses of the station interior, and No 321441 is the leading unit of the train in Platform 9. The cab road can be seen beyond Platform 10 to the left.
H. Bocking/Author

LIVERPOOL STREET

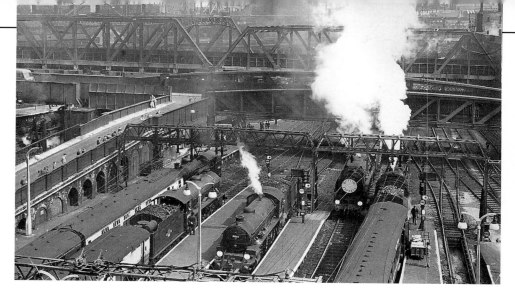

Then: 14 June 1958

Liverpool Street has always been a distinctive station, for many years divided into the west and east sides by the longer Platforms 9 and 10 used by the Norwich services. Today, the apparent distinction is minimal, but Platform 10 which incorporates the cab road is still some distance from Platform 11. In this splendid view of the east side may be seen (from left to right) 'N7' 0-6-2T 69633 with the 'Broadsman' empty stock, 'B17' 4-6-0 61647 *Helmingham Hall* with the 10.44 to Clacton, 'B1' 4-6-0 No 61283 awaiting the next turn of duty, the Butlin Express arriving behind a 'Britannia', and a Class 4 2-6-0 with the 10.47 to Clacton.

Now: 24 September 1998

Forty years have passed, and a viewpoint from the Primrose Street bridge in the background of the 'Then' picture is needed to avoid the extensive rafting over of the station's east side. It is to this bridge that the cab road exits. This view shows No 321476 approaching with an up morning peak service, amidst the welter of overhead equipment and complex pointwork.
R. E. Vincent/Author

thence to Bishop's Stortford and on to Stansted Airport (reached by a single-track tunnel of 1 mile 184 yd), or towards Cambridge.

All these services are operated by West Anglia Great Northern Railway (WAGN). All run at 2tph except those to Chingford (3tph), while the local trains to Bishop's Stortford are extended to Stansted Airport only once per hour.

The main lines continue to Stratford which, with its many junctions, is the nerve centre of the network, and on to Ilford. Just west of the station, the so-called electric lines (those which were part of the original 1949 electrification) cross the fast lines on a flyover. The lines are paired throughout as fast lines and electric lines. Romford sees the branch to Upminster diverge. At Shenfield (20 miles), the four-track section ends.

A diveunder avoids the need for Southend branch trains to foul the main line in crossing movements, and the two track railway continues to Southend Victoria, throwing off the single-track branch to Southminster at Wickford. The Colchester main line continues to Chelmsford and Witham, the latter being the junction for the Braintree branch.

These services are operated by Great Eastern Railway, apart from the Norwich trains of Anglia Railways. There are six local Shenfield services per hour, one of which is extended to Southminster. The Southend branch has a 3tph service and on the main line Chelmsford has 4tph and Witham 3tph. One of the latter continues to Braintree.

In the Stratford area, the former Great Eastern branch to North Woolwich has a passenger service operated by Silverlink

Metro, currently 3tph or 2tph in peaks. North of the station complex there are routes to the Lea Valley, the North London line, and the Tottenham & Hampstead.

Freight traffic is heavy to and from the east coast ports, much of this reaching the Great Eastern via the North London line at Stratford.

Today, nearly all the network is electrified at 25kV ac; in earlier guises, 1,500V dc was applied between Liverpool Street and Shenfield and to Southend Victoria. This was later converted to ac. The exception is the North Woolwich branch, which retains its third rail dc electrification system.

New developments in the area are the Jubilee Line Extension, open in 1999, and a domestic and international station on the Channel Tunnel Rail Link when that is constructed. Also of direct relevance will be the CrossRail scheme. This is planned to link the inner suburban Great Eastern services from Shenfield (and, possibly, beyond) via a new large diameter tunnel to the local lines from Paddington to Reading, and from Marylebone to Amersham and Aylesbury.

London Underground's Central Line rises to the surface briefly at Stratford to provide cross-platform interchange with GE electric line services and there is also connection with the Docklands Light Railway which runs alongside the GE from the Bow area to Stratford. The only time that the Victoria Line trains appear on the surface is at Northumberland Park depot, which is next to the Lea Valley line in the area north of Tottenham Hale.

LIVERPOOL STREET

Then: 25 August 1948
The Liverpool Street pilot engine was always beautifully turned out as exemplified by 'J69' 0-6-0T No E8619 in the roads between No 10 (left) and No 9 (right) platforms. The locomotive was finished in apple green LNER livery, and highly polished at that.

Later: 10 September 1987
A pilot locomotive is no longer needed, though the tradition of spit and polish was kept to the last. One of the final occupants of that post was 350hp shunter 08833, in Great Eastern blue. The engine idles while the locomotive stands in Platform 1. In the late 1960s, Class 15 locomotive D8234 performed this task.
E. D. Bruton/Author

ROMFORD.

Then: 22 July 1977
The wooden platform alongside the GE main line holds the solitary Class 105 Cravens unit, which performs the Romford-Upminster shuttle duty. Although strictly part of the LT&S network, this service has for many years been operated from the Romford end, and there are no physical connections with either the Underground or the LT&S line at Upminster.

STRATFORD

Then: 21 July 1980
The Class 306 units were introduced in 1,500V dc guise with the delayed 1949 Shenfield electrification. Later converted to 25kV ac, they were still at work in the early 1980s. The original unit, No 306001, is seen leaving Stratford for Shenfield at the head of a two-unit formation. Other very similar Class 506 units were employed on the Manchester-Hadfield services, and these remained dc units throughout their lives.

Now: 24 September 1998
There is only a realigned up fast line, which has its own platform face, between the platform on which the photographer is standing and the down electric line. Great Eastern unit No 315815 is at the head of the approaching eight-car formation. The building to the left of the tower blocks is the Jubilee Line Extension terminus, which includes the platforms for the Silverlink North London services. *Author (2)*

Now: 24 September 1998
The electrification of this branch, one of the last lines to be so treated in the Great Eastern's London area, results in the use of Class 315 units.
No 315838 is today's performer. Use of the leading cars is minimal, since the entrance/exit from the platforms is at the other end at both termini, and substantially so at the one intermediate station of Emerson Park. A Class 321 passes on a down service. *Author (2)*

GIDEA PARK

Then: 20 May 1980
Another look at the Shenfield 1949 units, 30 years old when this picture was taken and still before such newfangled ideas as sliding doors could be seen on the Southern. Unit No 085 arrives at Gidea Park with an up working at the beginning of the evening peak.

BRENTWOOD

Then: 23 August 1968
One of the original Class 307 Southend units No 110, themselves also originally dc, hurries through the station on the up fast line on a Southend Victoria-Liverpool Street service. It is at the head of an eight-car formation.

Now: 24 September 1998
The Class 321 units are the principal trains used by Great Eastern for outer suburban work nowadays. No 321365 approaches as the shadows lengthen. The station lighting is new, but the scene is still familiar.
Peter Ashton/Author

Now: 24 September 1998
The vintage overhead mast has disappeared, seemingly needing no replacement. The Great Eastern service has No 315810 at its head, again shortly before the start of the evening peak. *Author (2)*

SHENFIELD

Then: 20 May 1980
Having just surmounted Brentwood bank, a freight headed by an unidentified Class 37 hurries through Platform 3 as the driver seeks to regain speed.

Now: 24 September 1998
The scene has changed relatively little, though the public address system loudspeaker is no longer circular! No 90148 is a Freightliner locomotive, with a well-loaded train of container flats in tow, bound for Felixstowe. The train will need to be re-engined at Ipswich as the line thence to Felixstowe is not electrified.
Author (2)

WITHAM

Then: 15 July 1984
The Class 309 Clacton express units were the only example of high-specification trains of Mk1 builds for multiple-unit working. As such, they served the railway and its customers well. Later, they carried the short-lived London and South East livery of brown with orange strip and seen here on No 309913 as the leading unit as it calls at Witham on the down journey.

Now: 24 September 1998
Driving Brake Standard Open No 9709 is one of the vehicles converted for that purpose from MkIIf open seconds. These are used by Anglia Railways and seen here at Witham with a Liverpool Street-Norwich service powered by a Class 86 in the rear. As a station, Witham has experienced little change. *Author (2)*

WICKFORD

Then: 20 May 1980
The Southminster branch train consisting of a Class 105 DMU waits in the up side bay while No 307207 arrives at the front of a Liverpool Street-Southend Victoria working.

Now: 24 September 1998
The station, looking very well cared for, sees No 321312 arrive with the 13.40 from Liverpool Street. Southminster is now served during off-peak hours by through trains of Class 315 units from London, with the bays in use in peak hours only.
Author (2)

WOODHAM FERRERS

Then: 23 March 1981
The station house dominates this view of the platform, while the level crossing gates and the disused platform on the right indicate that this was once a busier location.

Now: 24 September 1998
No 315816 substitutes electric power, while the bushes have done their best to obscure the house. The canopy has been cut back for electrical clearance reasons. The semaphore has gone, and the level crossing converted to an automatic open crossing (AOCL).
Author (2)

SOUTHMINSTER

Then: 23 March 1981
In pre-electrification days, most of the trappings of a country terminus remain. The goods shed has a loading gauge outside and a concrete post supports the shunting signal. A Class 104 unit provides the branch power and is stationed in the platform.

Now: 1 May 1995
The infrastructure shown in the 'Then' picture has now gone; all that is left is the nuclear flask siding and associated run-round. The station itself, with No 321344, is a remarkable carbon copy of Woodham Ferrers. The lighting is identical and the canopy has been cut back in the same manner. Even the station house appears to have been built to the same design. *Author (2)*

STRATFORD LOW LEVEL

Then: 16 February 1957
From the North Woolwich branch, trains could proceed either towards the North London line or the Lea Valley and Temple Mills. The diverging point was Fork Junction, immediately to the north side of the GE main line. Here, LMS Ivatt 2-6-0 No 43024 takes the North London option.

SOUTHEND VICTORIA

Then: 11 January 1969
The long-departed Class 15s were based for most of their existence on the Great Eastern. D8228 is seen with an up parcels service in today's Platform 2.

Now: 4 November 1998
Unit No 321328 is in the same platform. Though the centre release road has gone, the overhead supports and what can be seen of the station building confirm that the location is the same. *Peter Ashton (2)*

Now: 29 September 1998
The site of Fork Junction can be glimpsed from Stratford Low Level platforms with the use of a telephoto lens. It is seen here with No 313014 approaching, bound for North Woolwich. The other line diverged to the right in this picture.
R. C. Riley/Author

CUSTOM HOUSE

Then: 30 August 1979
The Class 105 units provided the local service between North Woolwich and Stratford, albeit that it was extended with diesel power as seen here to Camden Road. Beyond Custom House, passenger operations latterly used the former down line only. A twin unit is approaching the signalbox, and the signalman is making his way over the foot crossing to receive the single line token from the driver.

SILVERTOWN

Then: 1 March 1977
Shortly after the passenger services had been reduced to single track, a Derby three-car unit forms a North Woolwich-Tottenham Hale service on a dismal day. The factory in the background is that of Tate & Lyle.

Now: 29 September 1998
The line now boasts third rail electrification, only the signalbox base survives and the semaphores are now colour lights. On the other side of the adjacent road there are now substantial trees. A Class 313 unit from North Woolwich to Richmond approaches. *Author (2)*

Now: 29 September 1998
The station, with its extremely narrow platforms on a cramped site, has been rebuilt in modest style, and the other platform and footbridge totally removed. Apart from the sugar factory, the only recognisable feature surviving is the Belisha beacon! *Author (2)*

SILVERTOWN

Then: 1 March 1977
The second track through the tunnel from Custom House below the dock entrance was still then used to service the Silvertown Tramway, which ran alongside the road westwards from Silvertown for a mile or so. No 08207 brought a daily trip from Temple Mills and shunted the sidings at the various Tramway premises. It is seen here waiting for the crossing gates to be opened.

Now: 29 September 1998
The crossing gates remain and are, if anything, smarter than before. But that is all. Railway freight traffic has long since ceased; further along, the former Tramway has been converted to a pedestrian and cycle route.
Author (2)

HACKNEY DOWNS

Then: 9 June 1960
With overhead line equipment already largely in place, LNER Thompson Class L1 2-6-4T No 67739 is hauling the 17.21 Hertford East-Liverpool Street service.

Now: 24 September 1998
A slightly wider angle shows all four platforms at this important junction; the Enfield lines are on the left, the Chingford lines on the right. Unit No 315851 is ready for departure for Liverpool Street on the left, and 317340 on the right.
H. F. Wheeller/Author

WALTHAMSTOW CENTRAL

Then: Undated, *c*1957
The location of this picture showing GE Class N7/2 0-6-2T No 69680 and a train of Quint-Arts (five articulated suburban carriages) is uncertain, but is included here to show the typical Great Eastern train which the 1960 Chenford electrification replaced. The arched platform awnings were also a Great Eastern feature.

Now: 24 April 1997
No 315854 arrives at Walthamstow Central with a Chingford-Liverpool Street service at one of the relatively few stations which still retain their awnings. *Author's Collection/Author*

TOTTENHAM HALE

Then: 5 October 1974
The bridge carries the A503 Ferry Lane across the railway immediately to the south of Tottenham Hale station. The incident pictured was the result of a burst water main, which demonstrated quickly that the ground is higher at the north end of the station platforms!

CHINGFORD

Then: 26 April 1986
The 12.41 ex-Liverpool Street arrives at Chingford in the charge of Class 305 No 422. Nos 445/9 can be seen, with others in the sidings.

Now: 27 June 1998
The arriving service is now No 315861, with No 317344 in the sidings. The overhead, the trackwork and even the carriage washer appear to have altered not at all. The notice to drivers on the carriage washer approach reads '3mph. Close doors and windows'.
Dr Martin Higginson (2)

Now: 29 September 1998
With no worries about water in the traction motors, refurbished unit No 317649 accelerates away from the station towards Liverpool Street. To the left can be seen the route of the former Lea Valley goods lines.
Author (2)

BROXBOURNE

Then: 3 October 1980
The King's Lynn services used to be in the hands of Class 37 locomotives and work, as seen here, to Liverpool Street. The early evening train is seen passing Broxbourne signalbox, a typical structure of its time now almost 40 years ago.

Now: 29 September 1998
The displacement of the Class 322 units from the Stansted Express resulted in the upgrading of Class 317 units. No 317655 is seen here in new WAGN livery. *Author (2)*

BISHOP'S STORTFORD

Then: 10 November 1974
An unidentified Class 37 heads a King's Lynn train into the station past Bishop's Stortford South box. This is now a fringe box to Harlow, but all will change with Railtrack's West Anglia Route Modernisation (WARM).

SAWBRIDGEWORTH

Then: 3 October 1980
The 19 Class 305/2 units were built for the North East London outer suburban services. Unit No 501 arrives with a train for Bishop's Stortford, the then extent of electrification.

Now: 29 September 1998
No 317651 in almost precisely the same position is for Stansted Airport, but the level crossing has been converted to automatic half barriers and the signalbox demolished. Tree growth hides much of the buildings behind, and the present scene is altogether less appealing. *Author (2)*

Now: 29 September 1998
No 317655 hurries into the station with a Stansted Airport train. The three platforms here are staggered, with the normal down single-faced platform further north and behind the photographer. *Author (2)*

WARE

Then: Undated, *c*1955
LNER N7/5 0-6-2T No 69652 arrives with a down service for Hertford North. Ware never had a second platform, all traffic being dealt with at the one shown on the north side of the line.

Now: 29 September 1998
The remains of the goods yard are overgrown but, as can be seen, the platform has been extended considerably beyond the end of the canopy. The signalbox has been demolished and replaced with a box next to the level crossing at the other end of the station. The adjacent small building remains. No 315859 arrives with a train for Hertford East.
Author's Collection/Author

HERTFORD EAST

Then: 14 September 1978
Class 305/1 unit No 420 passes the smart signalbox and enters Platform 1. This is another installation featuring searchlight signals.

Now: 29 September 1998
The Class 305 is replaced by No 315859, and Platform 2 is now preferred for normal use. Apart from the short siding on the right having been removed and a building behind the box, change is negligible.
Author (2)

The Great Northern

King's Cross of 1852 took its name from the statue of the late King George IV which previously occupied a site at the crossroads formed by Gray's Inn Road, Euston Road, Pentonville Road and Caledonian Road. This, the terminus of the Great Northern Railway, consisted of a number of separate parts. Those which survive today are the main train shed with its eight platforms, architect Lewis Cubitt, and the first suburban station on the west side with three more platforms. The further sprawl of suburban facilities, and the York Road platform on the up side, were abandoned when the connections to the Widened Lines were severed and efforts concentrated on the Great Northern & City services from Finsbury Park to Moorgate. These latter were inaugurated in 1976.

The whole of the Great Northern in this area is electrified at 25kV ac, apart from the tunnel section from Drayton Park to Moorgate which is third rail. This requires the use of dual voltage Class 313 units, which change power supplies while stationary at Drayton Park.

The main line itself is four-tracked apart from the two tracked section over Welwyn Viaduct, through Welwyn North station and the two tunnels. Tracks are paired by direction, and up direction suburban trains gain the west side platforms at the terminus by use of a flyover. Another flyover groups the terminating inner suburban trains on the west side of Welwyn Garden City station. Most stations in the suburban area consist of a pair of island platforms, which thus provide access to all running lines if so required.

The Hertford loop diverges at Alexandra Palace, rejoining the main line at Langley Junction, south of Stevenage. Both of these are grade separated junctions. There are nowadays no branches used by the passenger businesses, but freight connections are maintained to and from the North London line.

Trains on the Great Northern face a steady 1 in 200 climb out of King's Cross, in the course of which they pass through the tunnels outside King's Cross at Gasworks, Copenhagen, Wood Green, Barnet, Hadley Wood South and North, Potters Bar, also Welwyn South and North. The longest of these is Potters Bar, at 1,214yd. There is one long tunnel on the Hertford branch, Ponsbourne Tunnel (1 mile 924yd), south of Bayford.

Main line train services are provided by Great North Eastern Railway (GNER), with service frequencies typically as follows:
- 1tph Edinburgh/Glasgow Central
- 1tph Newcastle
- 1tph Leeds

Local services are offered by West Anglia Great Northern Railway (WAGN):
- 2tph Peterborough
- 4tph Cambridge, 1tph extended to King's Lynn
- 3tph Moorgate to Welwyn Garden City
- 3tph Moorgate to Hertford North, 1tph extended to Letchworth.

Traffic is growing, and some resolution of the Welwyn area bottleneck is being sought, but that can be achieved only at great cost. Another difficult area is Hitchin, where there is a flat crossing of the main line for Cambridge branch trains.

A park-and-ride facility has been considered at Hadley Wood by GNER. This would be aimed at attracting long-distance passengers who have access to the nearby M25, rather than the relatively short-distance traffic into London. At present, selected GNER trains call at Stevenage, 27.5 miles from King's Cross.

The advent of Thameslink 2000 will allow the outer suburban WAGN services to be diverted away from the present suburban platforms and back to the Widened Lines, thence to City Thameslink. Quite how many could be so redirected remains open to conjecture; there is a balance to be struck with the present Thameslink trains from the Midland line, the effects of traffic growth to be considered, and the interests of other operators who might wish to use some of the capacity. The latter could perhaps include BAA, who might use the Widened Lines to offer a Heathrow-Gatwick service via central London. Other airport interests include Luton and, possibly, Stansted. Moorgate thus seems set to be the terminus of the WAGN inner suburban services for the foreseeable future.

KING'S CROSS

Then: March 1962
No 67797 was one of the dozen or so King's Cross-allocated Thompson 'L1' 2-6-4Ts. The locomotive is seen here backing onto a train in the then Platform 8.

Now: 8 November 1997
The unique Class 89 locomotive was built at Crewe Works to a Brush design in 1987. It was retired, hurt, but survived and has been reinstated by its present owners GNER to help meet their power shortage. No 89001 was photographed leaving with the 08.10 to Leeds. *Author (2)*

KING'S CROSS

Then: 31 January 1959
The Great Northern received five of the first batch of 10 English Electric 1Co-Co1 2,000hp Class 4 diesels; the others went to the Great Eastern. Here is the first GN machine, No D201, after arrival in the then Platform 5 (now 4) with the 09.55 from Newcastle.

Now: 11 September 1998
Three Driving Brake Vans from GNER MkIV sets stand in Platforms 2, 3 and 4. The station train shed has changed little, though the footbridge in the background now has stairs only to Platform 1 (right) and the present Platform 8. There has of course been the addition of 25kV ac equipment.
M. Mensing/Author

KING'S CROSS

Then: 1959
The 10 Modernisation Plan 'Baby Deltics', later Class 23, were not a success. The first to be delivered, No D5900, arrives with an outer suburban working consisting of a mixed rake of BR and LNER stock.

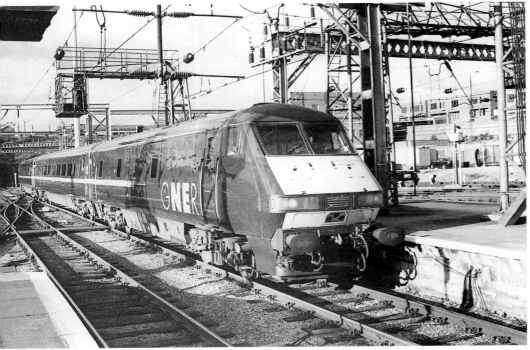

Now: 11 September 1998
The 10.00 from Glasgow Central arrives with Driving Brake Van No 82212 leading on entry into Platform 7. The present dominance of the overhead equipment is striking. *P. F. Winding/Author.*

KING'S CROSS

Then: Undated, *c*1964
The English Electric prototype 2,700hp diesel-electric locomotive No DP2 of 1962 became, effectively, a forerunner of the Class 50 design. Both incorporated the 16CSVT engine, but DP2 used what was, in effect, the last of the production Deltic bodies. It is seen here leaving with the Sheffield Pullman.

KING'S CROSS

Then: Undated, *c*1965
The Class 46 locomotives were regularly but not frequently seen in King's Cross. Here, Nos D176 (left in Platform 7) and D178 (right in Platform 8) will form services down the East Coast main line and to West Yorkshire respectively. The gaggle of 'spotters' are in their customary places.

Now: 11 September 1998
While the GNER Class 92 locomotives usually run 'nose first' they can be used 'blunt end first' if the occasion arises. An unidentified class member will depart shortly with the 15.30 to Newcastle. The location is recognisably the same.
Ian Allan Library/Author

Now: 11 September 1998
The clearance of the old signalbox which dominated the view from the platform ends did allow substantial rearrangement of the tracks in the short distance thence to Gasworks Tunnel. Indeed, from this view it is difficult to believe that the box once stood in line with the ends of the island platform which houses the central station roof supports. WAGN's No 317342 departs with the 10.21 to Peterborough. *Real Photos/Author*

KING'S CROSS

Then: 23 June 1949
Mainstay of the Great Northern suburban in steam days were the Class N2 0-6-2Ts, complete with their condensing gear and the Quad-Art sets of rolling stock. No 69506 heads a failed sister with a service for Hertford North out of Platform 16. Many passengers were left behind.

More then: 23 September 1950
A turntable was accommodated between the running lines and Gasworks Tunnel (left), while York Road platform for the Moorgate services can be seen in the background. Class A2/3 No 60523 *Sun Castle* is being turned.

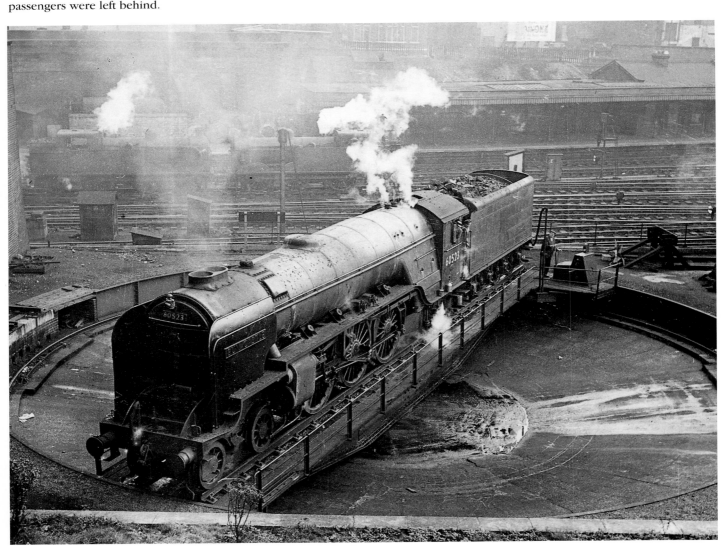

KING'S CROSS

Then: 29 July 1976
The short 57ft BR suburban coaching stock was used on the GN due to Widened Lines limitations. Here, in the morning peak, Class 31s take a train down from York Road to Moorgate (*right*) and empties out of the suburban station (*left*).

Now: 9 June 1998
In this picture, a GNER express is seen on the right, though not bound for Moorgate! WAGN No 365535 is arriving with the 16.06 from Ely. There is no change in the buildings above the tunnel mouth.
Dr Martin Higginson (2)

Now: 11 September 1998
This scene of desolation is from the top of Gasworks Tunnel, looking down onto the previous loco area (right), with the suburban station in the distance. *C. C. B. Herbert/ Ian Allan Library/Author*

KING'S CROSS

Then: 22 October 1977
The GN Suburban electrification diverted the inner suburban services from Finsbury Park to Moorgate and made much of the west side infrastructure redundant. In this picture, from left, the old Platforms 13-16 are all devoid of track; Platform 16 was the route up from the Widened Lines via the Hotel Curve. For the time being, the Parcels roads remain. St Pancras can be seen in the background.

Now: 11 September 1998
Most of the area has now been cleared and converted to light industrial use or for car parking. However, Platform 13 on the left, now No 11, has been reinstated; the capacity available for WAGN outer suburban traffic was found to be insufficient.
Nigel Hunt/Author

BETWEEN GASWORKS AND COPENHAGEN TUNNELS

Then: 15 July 1975
'Deltic' No 55003 *Meld* storms out of King's Cross with a full length train of air-conditioned MkIId coaches; no high speed flyer about this one. The North London line in those days was still carrying trains for Broad Street, and a Class 501 unit from Richmond may be seen crossing the viaduct. A Class 31 coasts down towards the terminus with an outer suburban set. Early signs of remodelling may be seen to the right of the express.

Now: 11 September 1998
No 313039 takes the up fast route towards King's Cross as a Class 91 approaches with the 11.30 to Newcastle. By now, all lines in sight have been electrified at 25kV ac. The slow lines on the right are still descending to the same level as the fast lines, following their crossing of the fast lines at the northern end of Copenhagen Tunnel. *Author (2)*

NORTH OF COPENHAGEN TUNNEL

Then: 15 July 1975
This is a typical consist for an outer suburban service in those days. No 31219 leaves the tunnel in the evening peak with a Cambridge service.

Now: 11 September 1998
Rather than being used for access to King's Cross goods only, the rebuilt flyover carries up direction suburban traffic clear of the fast lines as all enter the tunnel. No 365541 on the 12.15 'Cambridge Flyer' to King's Cross is gaining height for this purpose.
Author (2)

HARRINGAY WEST

Then: 4 June 1970
Beyond Finsbury Park, expresses begin to get into their stride, exactly as Class 47 No 1506 is doing on the down fast line approaching Harringay with a Grimsby/Cleethorpes service. The photograph was taken from the side of the box, as the rodding bears witness.

FINSBURY PARK

Then: 23 July 1979
This less than appealing entrance was hardly adequate for a busy Underground and BR station, but it was the result of the postponed and then abandoned elements of the LT New Works Programme 1935-40. This accounted also for the brickwork on the left. However, this picture was taken a quarter century after the event, and there was little excuse for allowing the situation to continue for that length of time. An empty HST set moves slowly through the station on its way from Bounds Green to King's Cross and commencing service.

Now: 15 October 1998
A new station entrance (right) plus bus station area has now obliterated the old eyesore. The (suffix) C registration Routemaster on Route 19 has seen it all. *Author (2)*

Now: 11 September 1998
The box site is now vacant, the semaphores have gone and the line is electrified. However, this is an HST set, used to reach those parts of the network electrics cannot. The train is the 14.00 King's Cross to Aberdeen, first stop York. This is 188.5 miles in 109min, average 104mph. Not bad for a 20-year-old piece of kit.
P. H. Groom/Author

WOOD GREEN, NOW ALEXANDRA PALACE

Then: 14 September 1978
In the early days, HST power cars were numbered as diesel units rather than as locomotives. No 254021 heads the 16.00 King's Cross-Edinburgh 'Talisman' through the station. This was before the days of the East Coast main line electrification.

Now: 14 November 1998
A viewpoint a little further down the platform shows what at first appears to be a curious piece of OHLE, but reality is less exciting. No 365520 is in charge of the 10.21 King's Cross to Peterborough. *Author (2)*

NEW SOUTHGATE

Then: 21 October 1961
The closure of the Midland & Great Northern Joint on 28 February 1959, almost in its entirety, left a fleet of Cravens multiple-units — ordered but not yet delivered — homeless. Now, why else should the Great Northern suburban be lumbered with vehicles that had only two slam doors per side, and insufficient power to be entrusted with peak hour services climbing up the Hotel Curve at King's Cross? Well, they would do as a stopgap, as the GN was about to be electrified, wasn't it? 18 years later, it was! One of the infamous Class 105s enters the station with the 12.39 Welwyn Garden City to King's Cross.

NEW SOUTHGATE

Then: 14 September 1978
No 312018 hurries through the fire-damaged station on the up fast with the 16.35 Royston to King's Cross.

Now: 11 September 1998
Almost exactly 20 years on, No 365532 follows its predecessor with the 14.15 Cambridge to King's Cross. The station has been selectively demolished, and appears to have been made good with the minimum of expenditure. *Author (2)*

11 September 1998
The Friern Barnet Road bridge is unchanged, though the sidings on the right have been lifted. The line is also electrified, for the benefit of No 317854, seen here approaching with the 13.54 Cambridge-King's Cross stopping service.
M. Mensing/Author

BARNET TUNNELS, OAKLEIGH PARK

Then: 5 April 1959
Class 40 No D208 pounds up the 1 in 200 gradient on the down fast with the 10.00 King's Cross to Edinburgh, the 'Flying Scotsman'. Of interest are the semaphore distants, which are on suspended brackets to allow train drivers to site them as they approach through the 605yd tunnels.

Now: 11 September 1998
Years later, the telegraph poles have gone and vegetation growth has covered the cutting sides. No 365521 forms the 17.05 King's Cross-Peterborough. *Author (2)*

OAKLEIGH PARK

Then: 5 March 1960
Classes 22, 23, 24, 26, 31... Finsbury Park had allocations of them all. One of the shorter stayers was the Class 24, with No D5052 seen here arriving with a down evening peak service.

Now: 11 September 1998
The down goods line has gone, the station buildings and canopies have been remodelled and cut back respectively, and the line has of course been electrified. No 313042 is arriving with a Moorgate-Welwyn Garden City local service. *Author (2)*

OAKLEIGH PARK

Then: 28 August 1961
A Hull-King's Cross service is headed by LNER Thompson Class A1 Pacific No 60158 *Aberdonian* on the up fast line. In those days, Oakleigh Park nameboards carried the additional information 'for East Barnet'.

Now:11 September 1998
No 365540 passes under a rebuilt and raised footbridge with the 15.42 Peterborough to King's Cross, and the customary 25kV has of course been added. *Author (2)*

NEW BARNET

Then: 16 September 1957
Now, that really is a train! LNER Gresley 'A4' Pacific No 60015 *Quicksilver* is at the head of the inaugural run of the 'Fair Maid', the 07.50 King's Cross to Edinburgh. Interestingly, this departure was described as 'early morning' in days before InterCity had even been thought about.

Now: 14 November 1998
The same scene with New Barnet in the background can just be discerned from this rather higher and more distant viewpoint. A Class 91-hauled GNER train forms the 16.20 King's Cross to Leeds.
Author's Collection/Author

HADLEY WOOD, GREENWOOD

Then: September 1952
The two-track section between Greenwood and Potters Bar of 2.5 miles was always a difficult operating feature of the Great Northern. LNER Gresley Class V2 2-6-2 No 60950 passes Greenwood box with the up Yorkshire 'Pullman', and the toes of the points which restore the four track section are just visible.

More then: 5 May 1970
Widening was carried out in the late 1950s, and this view of a 'Deltic'-hauled express on the up fast shows how the new Hadley Wood South Tunnel was bored on the west side and the realignments which were necessary. Originally, the two fast lines only would have passed through the old tunnel. Greenwood box would have been about two-thirds of the way down the train, on the left-hand side.

Now: 14 November 1998
No 365532 approaches on the up slow line with the 15.15 Peterborough to King's Cross. Electrification is evident, and the whole appears to be a mature setting — as indeed it should, nearly 40 years after the widening took place.
J. Davenport/Author (2)

POTTERS BAR

Then: Undated *c*1954
The widening included Potters Bar station (left) and the railway bridge over the road immediately to the south of the station. 'V2' 2-6-2 No 60909 is pictured amongst the civil engineering works.

Now: 15 October 1998
The station car park entrance is on the left, and a Class 313 unit on a down evening peak service can be seen in the down slow platform. The road is rather busier than the earlier picture might have suggested, while very substantial tree growth has replaced some of the site works.
Author's Collection/Author

BROOKMANS PARK

Then: 5 August 1976
In Rail Blue days and in the last months of diesel-unit operation, a Class 105 twin leaves the station with a King's Cross-Hitchin service.

Now: 15 October 1998
Changes to this scene since have been negligible, other perhaps than the loss of the barrow crossing. No 313045 is forming a Moorgate-Welwyn Garden City service. *Author (2)*

WELWYN SOUTH TUNNEL

Then: 25 March 1989
Only 286yd separate the two Welwyn tunnels, and in this brief interlude No 91001 emerges from Welwyn South with the 13.20 King's Cross to Leeds. In those days, full InterCity livery was *de rigueur*.

Now: 15 October 1998
The scene has become a little more overgrown, but No 91016 is heading the 16.30 departure from King's Cross to Leeds. GNER livery has been applied, as to the rest of this fleet, with a considerable change in appearance. *David Percival/Author*

KNEBWORTH

Then: 25 July 1964
Looking northwards from the station, the wide and trimmed cutting sides see Class 47 No D1547 approaching with an up local service on the slow line, while Class 40 No D385 rattles past on the down fast with a fast freight for Aberdeen.

Now: 15 October 1998
From a viewpoint at the end of the platform between the dow[n] and the down fast lines, the forestry has grown to the extent t[hat] distant bridge is only partially visible. There is also considerab[le] housing on the east side and, of course, electrification. An HS[T] brings the 'Northern Lights' 09.55 Aberdeen to King's Cross s[outh at] speed. *David Percival/Author*

STEVENAGE

Then: 28 December 1971
The decision was made to replace the existing Stevenage station with a new construction on a site to the south. This would also allow Stevenage to replace Hitchin as the calling point for longer distance services. Class 47 No 1996 passes the new site after clearance had begun with the 09.01 Cleethorpes to King's Cross.

Now: 15 October 1998
The result was a four-platform station consisting of two islands, with a centrally placed bridge for access and station facilities. The 'new' station was opened on 23 March 1973 and is thus now more than 25 years old. *P. R. Foster/Author*

BAYFORD

Then: 8 April 1984
Perhaps the quietest of GN suburban stations, the view here is from the down platform looking south towards Ponsbourne Tunnel. No 313033 is leaving with the 12.59 (Sundays) Hertford North to Moorgate, in the days before Moorgate services were diverted to King's Cross at weekends.

Now: 15 October 1998
Passenger facilities have since sadly diminished. There is a basic shelter on each platform, but everything else has been demolished. An intending customer is faced with intimidatory notices about penalty fares, but there are no means whatsoever of obtaining any form of ticket. Not that it seems to be necessary, since any on-train staff are noticeable by their non-appearance, and there are no barrier checks anyway. The one bright spot is a notice outside the station, directing those arriving to the nearest pub, which is out of sight.
John C. Baker/Author

HERTFORD NORTH

Then: 14 January 1984
One in three of the Hertford North services continue beyond to Stevenage and to Letchworth where they terminate. No 313055 is on an up working to Moorgate and is in Platform 1.

Now: 15 October 1998
The 12.52 Moorgate to Letchworth has just arrived in Platform 2 at Hertford North, formed of unit No 313046. New lamp standards have been erected, but overall there are few differences. Terminating trains mostly use the bay on the left, Platform 3. *Michael Collins/Author*

The Midland Railway

By anybody's standards, St Pancras is an imposing station, fronted by Sir George Gilbert Scott's Victorian Gothic hotel complete with its soaring pinnacles, great clock tower and huge arches. With over 500 rooms, and exceedingly lavish decoration, it has not been used as a hotel since 1935.

The station was opened in 1868 as the terminus of the Midland's new line from Bedford. This was the company's solution to the chronic overcrowding problems from which the Midland was suffering due to its use of Great Northern tracks. The company gained access to the GN via its now long-closed line from Bedford to Hitchin.

The train shed was designed by the company's consulting engineer W. H. Barlow, with a spectacular roof consisting of one 240ft span of iron and glass and no intermediate supporting pillars; at its apex, it is 100ft high. Clearly a success, the design was replicated 12 years later at Manchester Central, with a slightly smaller span of 210ft.

Today, St Pancras is used well below its capacity; although electrified, its six present platforms are frequented only by the diesel HST trains of Midland Main Line (MML). The whole of the suburban Thameslink service network avoids the terminal and takes the Widened Lines route to Farringdon. Here, the dual voltage electric units mostly lower their pantographs and proceed via City Thameslink to Blackfriars and beyond, though a peak service is retained to the Moorgate terminus. Thameslink routes take these services to Gatwick Airport and Brighton, and also to the Wimbledon and Sutton loop.

The Midland line is four-tracked today to a point beyond Bedford. The basic MML operation consists of an hourly Nottingham and an hourly Sheffield via Derby service from St Pancras. Some of these call at Luton (30 miles). There are also four Thameslink trains per hour calling at St Albans and stations to Bedford, four all stations to Luton, and an hourly fast from Farringdon calling at King's Cross Thameslink, Luton and Bedford only.

Midland tracks are paired as fast lines and slow lines, the latter being on the eastern side of the formation. The standard station arrangement sees a central island platform between the up fast and down slow, with two side platforms. The only tunnels of substance are the Belsize tunnels (slightly more than one mile) and Elstree, 1,058yd long.

Future plans by MLL foresee substantial service increases with the addition of diesel units to the rolling stock fleet, while St Pancras is intended also as the London terminus of the Channel Tunnel Rail Link. The BAA link from Heathrow to St Pancras is to use the line from Acton via Dudding Hill Junction to join the Midland at Cricklewood, and Thameslink trains are using the new Luton Airport Parkway station from its 1999 opening. The range of Thameslink destinations south of the Thames may be much increased by the planned Thameslink 2000 upgrade, but Moorgate will cease to be served by the Widened Lines.

Essentially a Midland branch, the Tottenham & Hampstead line offers a connection from the Kentish Town area through to Barking. A passenger service on this line, run by Silverlink Metro, consists of a 2tph service calling at all stations from Gospel Oak (with connections to the North London line) to Barking. It is operated presently with first generation Class 117 diesel units, which leave much to be desired. By 1999, together with the Class 205 units on the Uckfield branch, these were the only Modernisation Plan diesel units still being used within 30 miles of London.

Freight, especially aggregates, remains an important part of Midland traffics. However, the flows of coal from pits in the Midlands and North, southwards to Cricklewood, are no longer.

ST PANCRAS

Then: 13 September 1983
Passengers make for the barrier having just arrived on the smartly turned out HST at Platform 3.

Now: 20 October 1998
InterCity livery has given way to that of Midland main line, though in this case the arriving train is that on the right in Platform 4. The power cars are Nos 43045 (left) and 43059 (right); the latter formed the 06.22 from Sheffield. Fewer passengers does not imply diminishing business, but merely the photographer's speed in reaching the equivalent vantage point. *Author (2)*

ST PANCRAS

Then: April 1986
In the days when ticket barrier checks were undertaken and when Midland suburban services still used St Pancras to terminate, No 317310 will shortly be departing for Bedford.

Now: 20 October 1998
The location is the same, but it is up to the passenger to ensure that he is on the right train and holds the correct ticket. Passengers board the 09.30 to Sheffield. *Author (2)*

ST PANCRAS

Then: Undated, c1959
Platform 7 sees Stanier 'Black 5' 4-6-0 No 44658 at the buffer stops. According to the blackboard notice, this will be the '6.40pm to Nottingham, Alfreton, Chesterfield, Sheffield'. The porter on the left, with his trolley, is another long-gone aspect of railway work.

Now: 20 October 1998
HST power-car No 43082 'Derbyshire First' in the same spot. The walls have been cleared of the poster boards and a yellow line added parallel to the platform edge, but little else is needed to update the scene.
Author (2)

ST PANCRAS

Then: 25 May 1948
These three photographs have been selected to show the changing scene over the years in this magnificent station. Each features a different form of traction, but none reflects the present day. 'Jubilee' 4-6-0 No 45694 *Bellerophon* has been decked out in green and is leaving Platform 3 with the 16.50 'Bradford Restaurant Car Express in Cream and Brown', according to the photographer. Of note is the semaphore signal, well under the roof.

Then, but in the electric era: 8 September 1984
The illuminated train shed shows up well on a Saturday night as Class 40 No 40122 prepares to work the 00.20 newspaper train to Derby from Platform 5.

Then, with an electric train: 27 April 1987
Midland Suburban Electric unit No 317340 is at the head of an eight-car formation in what might be termed the pure blue and grey livery before Network SouthEast spread everywhere. This is a departure for Bedford, in Platform 3.
E. D. Bruton/B. J. Beer/Author

ST PANCRAS

Then: Undated, *c*1952
Class 2P Midland Compound 4-4-0 No 41054 enters the station passing the large Midland signalbox on the eastern side with a local train.

Now: 20 October 1998
An HST set takes a similar route, but little more than the gasholders and the bridge girders remain. Overhead electrification seldom enhances the scene. *Author's Collection/Author*

ST PANCRAS

Then: July 1977
Class 45 No 45126 leaves with an early evening express for Sheffield. These were the days of air-conditioned comfort, but not yet the High Speed Train. The view was obtained from the old St Pancras churchyard.

Now: 11 November 1998
Encroaching vegetation has limited the views available, but a Midland Main Line HST set can be seen disappearing into the terminus. *Author (2)*

WEST HAMPSTEAD

Then: 1 December 1978
The Class 44/45/46s were the principal service providers on the Midland from the 1960s through to the early 1980s. No 45116, with a train for Nottingham, leaves the Finchley Road tunnels and approaches the station on the slow lines.

Now: 16 October 1998
A complete rearrangement of track layout, electrification and the construction of a supermarket on the right of the picture makes a considerable difference. An HST set forms the 16.30 St Pancras to Leeds. *Author (2)*

MILL HILL BROADWAY

Then: 6 August 1959
BR Standard Class 4 4-6-0 No 75043 pauses in mid-afternoon with an up local service on the fast lines, in the days when this consisted of an hourly service from Luton to St Pancras.

WEST HAMPSTEAD THAMESLINK

Then: 1 December 1978
The diesel units of Class 127 had hydraulic transmission and were thus of the Red Triangle coupling variety and non-standard. An up service is seen arriving on the slow lines, with the signalbox at the end of the island platform.

Now: 16 October 1998
The houses behind the station have changed little, but the box has been replaced by the West Hampstead power box controlling the whole of the 25kV electrified area. No 319180 is the lead unit on the 15.46 Luton to Sutton via Wimbledon. *Author (2)*

Now: 16 October 1998
The station was completely reconstructed with the building of the M1 Motorway, which passes alongside the east side of the station, or behind the wall in the background. Arriving passengers make their way out from the ticket office area via a car park beneath the motorway. This is as unpleasant as it sounds. No 319428 hurries through with the 09.57 Bedford to Brighton. *Author (2)*

ELSTREE & BOREHAMWOOD, SLOW LINES

Then: 17 May 1952
Ivatt Class 4 2-6-0 No 43049 emerges with a northbound Class 7 express freight. Such a train is not fully fitted with the continuous brake.

Now: 16 October 1998
An up Thameslink service formed of No 319186 leaves the station on the slow line with the 11.01 Luton to Sutton via Streatham.
C. R. L. Coles/Author

RADLETT

Then: 27 September 1978
No 25182 passes Radlett, a typical Midland Railway creation, with an up parcels train. All the vehicles are of BR origin, with none from the pre-Nationalisation companies or to their designs.

ELSTREE & BOREHAMWOOD, FAST LINES

Then: 12 October 1963
Class 46 No D149 leaves Elstree Tunnel with a fast freight bound for Derby; the slow line tunnels are beyond.

Now: 16 October 1998
The 11.00 St Pancras-Nottingham formed of a Midland Main Line HST set hurries north. The slim, tall tree is common to both pictures.
Brian Stephenson/Author

Now: 16 October 1998
Reconstruction at the beginning of the 1980s has resulted in a standard modern station. One necessity was to provided clearances for the then forthcoming electrification.
No 319369 is in charge of the 12.16 Luton to Sutton via Wimbledon as it leaves Radlett. *Author (2)*

RADLETT

Then: 27 September 1978
With the station building in the background, a Class 127 unit forms a St Pancras-Luton service in the rain. Part of the former goods yard area on the left has become a small car park.

Now: 16 October 1998
No 319363 is photographed in the same position with the 11.36 Sutton to Luton via Wimbledon. The growth of car parking in the intervening period has been phenomenal, and it extends further out of the picture. Demand is such that those approaching meet a notice telling them that there are no spare places. *Author (2)*

ST ALBANS CITY

Then: 26 July 1976
Class 45 No 45029 takes the slow
lines as it approaches St Albans City
with a train of hoppers. The platform
on the left is a repository for quite a
selection of barrows.

Now: 16 October 1998
The bay on the left has disappeared,
and the now disused signalbox seems
to be being prepared for removal. The
14.00 HST St Pancras to Nottingham is
approaching on the down fast line,
obscured partly by the lighting
column.

Now: 16 October 1998
The photographer had been hoping
that a freight would materialise, but
this did not happen until he had
returned to the platforms. EWS
No 60049 takes an aggregates train
through St Albans City on the down
slow line; the Midland is still an
important freight carrier.
Author (3)

HARPENDEN JUNCTION

Then: 27 September 1978
An unidentified Class 47 hauls a train of empty HAA coal hoppers north along the Midland main line, with semaphores very much still in evidence.

HARPENDEN JUNCTION

Then: 27 September 1978
No 45130 is the motive power for this St Pancras-Derby services, made up of a total of nine Mk1 vehicles. Harpenden Junction box is behind the fifth and sixth vehicles, and the junction was formerly a branch to Hemel Hempstead.

Now: 16 October 1998
This is the Sandite season, in which superannuated vehicles are taken round the system spreading a paste-like substance on the rails to assist adhesion. No 930078 is being propelled for this task northwards on the down slow line by a Class 319 unit. This vehicle started life as part of a South Tyneside electric unit. *Author (2)*

Now: 16 October 1998
The box and the semaphores have gone, and electrification masts have appeared. The 15.00 St Pancras to Nottingham is formed from a Midland Main Line HST set. *Author (2)*

LUTON MIDLAND ROAD

Then: September 1960
Well turned out Stanier Class 5 4-6-0 No 44984 arrives on the down slow line with the return Cricklewood-Derby milk tanks. This train ran as a Class 3, for perishable traffic allowed to travel at 90mph.

Now: 16 October 1998
The scene has changed entirely, with the land in the background ceasing to be used for railway purposes and the buildings demolished. The only link is the treeline, and the section above the second coach of the approaching No 319382 can be related to that above the first two milk tanks. Further similarities then become apparent.
John C. Baker/Author

KING'S CROSS, THAMESLINK

Then: 1978
The Widened Lines were never well used, and became less so after the withdrawal of the GN services in 1976. All that was then left was the occasional peak hour train from the Midland. The barren platforms are seen here, looking towards Moorgate, as a C stock train passes with a Whitechapel-Hammersmith working.

Now: 11 November 1998
The curve in the tracks (now of slab construction), the bridge in the background and indeed other buildings help place this picture of the present King's Cross Thameslink. The station is now linked in with the Underground tube lines, while 8tph may run to Blackfriars and beyond and 5tph to Moorgate. Patronage is thus considerably higher.
Dr Martin Higginson/Author

FARRINGDON

Then: 14 July 1969

The Widened Lines are now on the south side of the formation, Class 31 No D5625 breasting the gradient up from below the Metropolitan tracks. The train is empty stock for a Great Northern service. There is now no rail connection with the Metropolitan and the stabling siding on the left for a shunting locomotive to act as a banker is no longer required.

Now: 2 January 1998

Platform lengthening work has obscured much of the former infrastructure. No 319053 in the old 'grey' Thameslink livery arrives with a train for Sutton via Wimbledon. The line has also been electrified, first at 25kV ac and then at 750V dc. Services proceeding to or from Blackfriars make the changeover while stationary here. *Peter Ashton/Author*

MOORGATE

Then: Undated, *c*1962
An up morning peak service from the Midland line arrives behind Class 24 No D5092 in less than pristine condition. The platform too is completely devoid of shelter. A sister locomotive is about to attach itself to the rear of the train.

Now: 11 November 1998
Moorgate Widened Lines station is now below commercial development, and only two platforms are available for Thameslink (Nos 5 and 6). No 319365 forms the 17.01 to St Albans and No 319423 will be the 17.10 to Bedford. *Author's Collection/Author*

SOUTH TOTTENHAM

Then: 25 September 1982
A three-car Class 116 formation, in two different colour schemes, forms the 16.55 Gospel Oak to Barking service as it approaches. The bridge in the background carries the GE line between Stamford Hill and Seven Sisters on the Enfield branch. A connection to this line is hidden beneath the train.

Now: 24 April 1997
The Class 116 has become a Class 117 and reduced to two cars, and is seen here entering the station. It is operated by Silverlink Metro. Overhead electrification is provided for the use of WAGN's 11.13 Enfield Town to Stratford train on Mondays to Fridays. *Michael J. Collins/Author*

BLACKHORSE ROAD

Then: 19 May 1971
Despite the destination blind, the train of Class 116 cars is for Barking; in those days the service ran from Kentish Town rather than Gospel Oak as now. The station formed a not very convenient interchange with the Victoria Line of London Underground and it was necessary to cross Blackhorse Road itself, immediately behind the photographer. This is the view looking east.

Now: 7 November 1998
The old station has gone and the Class 117 unit No 117706 is passing all that remains of the slope down to the platforms on the left.

Now: 7 November 1998
However, Blackhorse Road station still exists. It was rebuilt in 1981 on the west side of that road, with the entrance linked into the Victoria Line ticket hall. This is the view looking east, with a Barking-Gospel Oak train arriving. *P. H. Groom/Author (2)*

The London & North Western Railway

The 'Premier Line', as the pre-Grouping company immodestly called itself, remains today as Britain's most major rail artery. The original Euston station was opened in 1837 and housed the first main line into London. That train shed was said to be unimpressive, but the whole was completely overshadowed by Philip Hardwick's Doric Arch at the main entrance. This monumental construction was an attempt by the Directors to give some indication of the significance of their railway, and to mark the beginning of a new era.

The West Coast main line was built between 1830 and 1850, and subsequently improved in the 1890 to 1920 period. It caters for about 2,000 trains per day. Electrification, first in the northwest, was extended to the London area in 1965, with accelerated timetables for the main line from 1966 and to the West Midlands in 1967. 'We're moving closer to the Heart of England' was the advertising theme from that period.

The railway is effectively four-tracked from its Euston terminus right through to Rugby, 82 miles from London. South of Watford Junction, the 'dc lines' alongside carry a local service from Euston, and London Underground Bakerloo Line services projected northwards from Queen's Park. Some of these services extend north as far as Harrow & Wealdstone.

The lines are paired as fast and slow lines, with the dc lines on the eastern side until a little south of Wembley Central, where a diveunder takes them to the west. There are numerous junctions, notably in the Willesden area which has links to the North London and West London lines. Both of these then provide further useful connections to the rest of the national network. One branch only survives today, that from Watford Junction to St Albans Abbey. Apart from the dc lines, the whole of the network described in the vicinity of the West Coast main line is electrified at 25kV ac.

There are lengthy tunnels at Primrose Hill (1,182yd), a couple of miles north of Euston, and at Watford (1 mile 55yd fast lines, 1 mile 230yd slow), with a short one at Northchurch, beyond Berkhamsted (349yd).

Service provision is primarily by Virgin Trains for the former InterCity network, and by Silverlink Train Services for the suburban services. Leaving Euston in each hour on Virgin are:
- 1tph to Manchester Piccadilly
- 1tph to Liverpool Lime Street
- 2tph to the West Midlands
- 1tph to Preston or beyond.

Several of these services call at Watford Junction.

Largely complementary to these services, Silverlink offers:
- 2tph to Birmingham New Street
- 2tph to Northampton
- 2tph to Milton Keynes Central.

Other passenger operators are North Western Trains with occasional forays from such places as Rochdale and Blackpool, Connex South Central with an hourly service from Gatwick Airport to Rugby via the West London line (this of course does not serve Euston), and the Anglo-Scottish sleeper services provided by ScotRail Railways. Virgin also offers very limited services from Brighton as part of its CrossCountry operation.

Silverlink Metro provides the non-radial services which centre on Willesden. These are the 3tph Richmond-North Woolwich, and the 2tph Willesden Junction-Kensington (Olympia)-Clapham Junction services. Both are busy sections of railway with a variety of traffics, and line occupation is at a premium. The North London line, which in times past had a city terminus at Broad Street, negotiates the heights of Hampstead with the aid of the 1,166yd Hampstead Heath Tunnel.

There is also heavy freight traffic: 55% of all freight trains operated nationally use a part of the WCML in their journeys.

The forthcoming upgrade of the West Coast main line by Virgin in conjunction with Railtrack will provide 14 standard paths per hour between Euston and Rugby and 140mph to Basford Hall (Crewe) by 2005. Tilting trains are needed to attain such performance. By 2002, London to Birmingham will take 76min at a maximum of 125mph, and by 2005 71min at a maximum of 140mph (beyond Willesden). Freight trains of up to 785m will be allowed, with a maximum container height of 9ft 6in. Performance specifications require 88% of trains to be on time or less than 6min late.

The remodelling of the Euston-Primrose Hill section started in 1998, and the new station throat arrangements will allow entry/exit to all platforms without conflicts. Silverlink trains will occupy the middle part of the station and Virgin the rest. Locomotive release facilities at Euston are effectively redundant for most purposes.

From Willesden to Milton Keynes, junctions between the pairs of tracks will be used only for contingencies and for maintenance requirements. Passengers will not be allowed access to platforms where 140mph trains will be passing.

The upgrade cost to Railtrack is £2.2 billion, with Virgin spending £1 billion on tilting trains.

On a much smaller scale, a new station on the West London line at West Brompton, for access to Earl's Court Exhibition Centre but also with interchange to London Underground, opened in 1999.

EUSTON

Then: May 1964
Demolition was well under way at this time. Stanier 'Black 5' 4-6-0 No 44866 is in Platform 3 with the 09.02 ex-Wolverhampton, while what became a Class 501 unit — then quite new — stands in Platform 4 with a dc lines service.

Now: 20 October 1998
The same platforms see Virgin Driving Brake Van No 82135 and, on the left and carrying Stansted Express livery, No 322481. The multiple-unit will form the 11.25 to Manchester Airport for North Western Trains. Together they demonstrate the lack of need for locomotive release facilities. *M. S. Welch/Author*

EUSTON

Then: Undated, *c*1960
An LMS '2P' 4-4-0 No 40646 is on empty stock duties at Euston's Platform 1; the driver looks as if he is ready to move off. The girders between the canopies were a distinctive feature of these platforms at 'the country end'.

Now: 1 September 1998
Electric locomotive No 87029 *Earl Marischal* is also on empty stock duties from Platform 2, as can be seen from the position of the marker lights. The scene is dominated by the access road which descends between Platforms 2 and 3, and Euston looks its usual dreary self. *Author's Collection/Author*

EUSTON

Then: 28 August 1952
'Princess' class '8P' No 46202 *Princess Anne* was rebuilt from the experimental 'Turbomotive' and is seen on its first trip before departure from Euston with the 08.30 to Liverpool Lime Street. Just over five weeks later, it was destroyed in the disastrous Harrow & Wealdstone collision. This picture was taken on the then somewhat primitive departure side of Euston.

EUSTON

Then: Undated, *c*1962
A 'Jubilee' class '6P5F' 4-6-0 No 45709 *Implacable* arrives in Euston. This is the view which the photographer of the '2P' (previous 'Then' picture) might have seen on turning round. While railways generally are efficient users of space, large terminal stations are indeed just that — large.

Now: 1 September 1998
Silverlink County unit No 321430 enters today's Euston with the 10.30 from Northampton. By extending the yellow doors livery onto the roof, the location of the doors is made easier to spot even when they are open.
Author's Collection/Author

Now: 20 October 1998
This Virgin Trains HST set, leading power car No 43121 *West Yorkshire Metropolitan County*, forms the 10.40 to Blackpool North and is preparing to leave Platform 15. The location is thus much the same.
Ian Allan Library/Author

EUSTON

Then: 17 November 1978
The 'AL6' fleet, today's Class 86s, has completed millions of journeys between London and Birmingham. This is a Liverpool train behind No 86239, leaving from one of the centre platforms of the station.

Now: 20 October 1998
Today's equivalent is represented by No 87032 *Kenilworth*, seen here before departure with the 11.05 to Liverpool Lime Street. There have been few changes; the parcels facility remains, and the ramp down to the platform can also be seen. *Author (2)*

PRIMROSE HILL

Then: 12 July 1979
With the best equipment of the day, No 87007 *City of Manchester* has a train of MkIII coaches behind it as the train approaches Primrose Hill Tunnel on the down fast line. The train is the 10.45 Euston-Glasgow Central.

Now: 1 September 1998
Same locomotive class, earlier coaching stock. No 87032 *Kenilworth* has a train of MkIIe/f stock behind as it forms the 15.15 Euston to Birmingham New Street. The wider angle lens shows the surrounding area to greater advantage, and some track removed in the centre part of the picture. *Author (2)*

PRIMROSE HILL

Then: 12 July 1979
The Class 310 75mph fleet monopolised the outer suburban operation in the early years. No 310092 makes for Euston at the head of an eight-car train over trackwork now abandoned.

Now: 1 September 1998
Royal Mail's fleet of 16 Class 325 four-car units work extensively to and from the Princess Royal Distribution Depot at Willesden. Here a 12-car formation will take the North London line route to run onto the East Coast main line. These units have dual 25kV ac and 750V dc electrification capability to maximise the area over which they may work unassisted. *Author (2)*

QUEEN'S PARK

Then: 5 July 1984
No 86208 *City of Chester* passes Queen's Park with an up express, as seen from the dc lines platforms. On the down/northbound platform nearest the camera there was 'an extended interval' in the service.

KILBURN HIGH ROAD

Then: June 1960
'Royal Scot' 4-6-0 No 46120 *Royal Inniskilling Fusilier* passes with a Euston-Northampton train on the down slow line. The platforms on other than the dc lines have long since gone.

Now: 27 October 1998
A Virgin-liveried down express, the 09.40 to Manchester Piccadilly is headed by No 90014. The dc lines are to the left of the picture. *Derek Cross/Author*

Now: 27 October 1998
Further screening work has effectively hidden the main line trains from view, though the roof of a Class 321 unit can be seen passing. The glass panels of the station roof have been covered selectively and some platform furniture has been replaced, but the station is still very much as it was. *Author (2)*

WILLESDEN JUNCTION

Then: 3 October 1977
No 86014 is the locomotive hauling a mixed rake of stock with examples from MkI, MkII and MkIII designs. This is an up working to Euston, passing the yard areas beyond the station area.

Now: 27 October 1998
The 'Now' viewpoint is a little further back. With the bridge in the foreground carrying the North London line to the high level station out of picture on right, an unidentified Virgin Trains service can be seen on the up fast line with a Driving Brake Van leading. A link between the two pictures can be made from the building above the Class 86 (Then) and that above the DBV/1st coach (Now). *Author (2)*

WILLESDEN JUNCTION

Then: 6 October 1980
A 1938 stock train from Elephant & Castle leaves for Stonebridge Park. London Underground operates over (what were then) BR tracks; the latter were responsible for the infrastructure and its maintenance. Also, BR fares applied.

WILLESDEN JUNCTION

Then: 3 October 1977
One of the then ubiquitous Class 501
units arrives in the low level platform
(the high level is behind) with a
Euston-Watford Junction train. The
appellation 'Willesden New Station'
for the signalbox is by now a trifle
outdated.

Now: 22 October 1998
The Bakerloo Line train of 1972 stock
has drawn up to the cameras which
display views of the platform to the
driver for use when he closes the
doors. Harrow & Wealdstone is the
destination of this train, which is now
the furthest extent reached by the
Underground. The signalbox has
gone. *Author (2)*

Now: 27 October 1998
No 313004 is still in Network
SouthEast livery as it departs with the
12.17 Euston-Watford Junction. The
Class 313 units are dual voltage, but
the up line seems to have acquired a
section with no electrification at all
compared with the earlier view. One
presumes that this is not long enough
to 'gap' any of the electric trains
which might use the line and thus
strand them with no access to current
supplies. *Author (2)*

SOUTH KENTON

Then: 28 August 1954
'Royal Scot' No 46106 *Gordon Highlander* heads a down Blackpool express of 16 vehicles, mostly of LMS vintage. The whole train is turned out in the then crimson and cream express livery, with a green locomotive.

Now: 27 October 1998
Nos 86637 and 86638 are Freightliner locomotives, seen heading north along the slow lines of the West Coast main line and leaving South Kenton in the distance behind them. The houses on the far side of the line are still there, but hidden behind the growth of bushes and trees. *Real Photos/Author*

SOUTH KENTON

Then and now: 27 October 1998
Directional street signs with the BR 'sausage' emblem were once commonplace, but they are a decided rarity nowadays. This well-worn example is teamed with a rather more modern sign giving a similar message. They may be found at the junction of Windermere Avenue and Grasmere Avenue. *Author*

NORTHWICK PARK (IN BACKGROUND)

Then: 26 August 1964
This fine study shows '8P' Stanier Pacific No 46239 *City of Chester* hauling the 08.05 Euston to Holyhead boat train. Use of these locomotives south of Crewe is about to cease, since the diagonal yellow band has been applied to the cab side signifying this restriction. Overhead wiring is in place, but not yet energised.

Now: 27 October 1998
The same location is not accessible today, so this picture was taken facing in the same direction from the footbridge in the background. Silverlink County's No 321430 is forming the 15.04 Euston to Milton Keynes Central. *P. J. Russell/Author*

KENTON

Then: August 1950
A Manchester Piccadilly to Euston express hurries under the Metropolitan and Great Central lines between Wembley Park and Harrow-on-the-Hill, on its way south. The locomotive is unrebuilt 'Royal Scot' No 46158 *The Loyal Regiment*.

Now: 27 October 1998
The lineside view is now completely obscured, so the photographer is forced to make use of the nearest overbridge. A 1972 stock Bakerloo Line train for Elephant & Castle is a less exotic substitute, but LUL corporate livery does stand out well in overcast (not to mention damp) conditions. The main bridge span still covers four tracks of the main line.
Derek Cross/Author

HARROW & WEALDSTONE

Then: 5 July 1984
An empty Class 501 unit on the up dc line approaches Harrow & Wealdstone, passing a 1938 stock Bakerloo Line train in one of the pair of sidings used by the Underground to stable trains temporarily. The down Watford line passes behind the box.

Now: 20 October 1978
The scene is repeated, but with substantial differences. Silverlink Metro No 313103 is in service, the Underground train has become 1972 stock and there is now only one siding, and the box has been closed and removed. The signalling has also been renewed. *Author (2)*

CARPENDERS PARK

Then: 7 September 1963
Class 40 diesels found maximum use on the West Coast; No D220 *Franconia* is heading the 15.55 Euston to Manchester Piccadilly. On the left, a 1938 stock southbound tube train is coming to a stop.

Now: 20 October 1998
Overhead line equipment has been erected, and the fourth rail still in position is redundant, due to Underground withdrawal north of Harrow. This is a Connex SouthCentral dual voltage unit No 319004. The train is the 15.37 Gatwick Airport to Watford Junction. *Peter Ashton/Author*

WATFORD HIGH STREET

Then: 6 April 1977
A 1938 stock train on the dc lines enters Watford High Street, the only station which is out of sight of the main line. Some Underground trains were stabled at the now closed Croxley depot overnight, but all are now kept at Stonebridge Park main depot or points further south.

CARPENDERS PARK

Then: 7 September 1963
The 15.16 Bletchley to Euston is formed of seven compartment vehicles powered by one of the last of the Class 24s, No D5145. The train is passing beneath what will become a signal gantry. Bletchley remains a depot, but its importance in service terms has long been eclipsed by Milton Keynes.

Now: 20 October 1998
Driving Brake Van No 82149 is at the head of the 14.30 Manchester Piccadilly to Euston; the gantry has been joined by all the overhead equipment. *Peter Ashton/Author*

Now: 20 October 1998
The vegetation has grown and the hut has gone, but the crossover between the tracks remains; it is for access to the Croxley Green branch. The signalling has also been renewed. Silverlink Metro's No 313019 is departing with the 15.05 Watford Junction to Euston. *Author (2)*

WATFORD JUNCTION

Then: 26 March 1953
An unidentified up express leaves
Watford Tunnel (on the fast lines)
behind Stanier 'Black 5' No 44837.

Now: 20 October 1998
Such locations are not accessible
today; the tunnel mouth is visible in
the distance, about 500yd from the
station platform on the down fast line.
Author's Collection/Author

KINGS LANGLEY

Then: 28 August 1948
The 08.55 Llandudno to Euston service passes on the up fast line behind Fowler 'Patriot' 4-6-0 No 45510. This was one of the few unnamed locomotives in the class. There is a substantial station building.

Now: 20 October 1998
Silverlink County runs a 2tph Milton Keynes Central to Euston service, calling at Kings Langley. This is the 13.13 departure, formed of unit No 321432. The station is very much 1950s reconstruction to a basic design, with some vandalism; the exit is from a subway leading to the down side (on left of picture), and thus below platform level. The platforms also seem to have been extended. Descending from the ramps at the south end now would put one immediately underneath the M25 motorway, which crosses the WCML on a high bridge. *E. D. Bruton/Author*

ST ALBANS ABBEY

Then: 28 July 1951
Ivatt Class 2 2-6-2T No 41275 is push-pull fitted and is seen after arrival at Abbey station from Watford Junction. The locomotive was built at Crewe the previous year, and the coach is a brand-new vehicle with a control compartment for reverse running, so the photographer proudly tells us. In other words, these were 'state of the art' branch line operations nearly half a century ago.

Now: 20 October 1998
The station has shrunk to a single platform with basic shelter, the line to Hatfield (not in pictures) has long since closed, and operation is one train working with no points or crossings. On the other hand, the line survives, has been electrified, and use of a three-car unit is deemed suitable for the traffic. (There aren't any shorter ones, anyway.) Silverlink Metro unit No 313121 awaits departure with the 11.36 to Watford Junction. *C. W. Footer/Author*

SOUTH ACTON

Then: 10 June 1978
This is very much the 'old railway', with wooden platforms, semaphores and 1950s design multiple-units. A Richmond-Broad Street train is arriving, this being the point where North London trains join the link from the Southern and the former Feltham marshalling yard. A fashion note for the benefit of graffito *cognoscenti*: the addition to the footbridge on the left reads 'Ban Tights, Bring Back Stockings' and on the right 'Stockings For Ever, Tights — Never!'

Now: 27 October 1998
Virtually everything in this picture is new, compared with 20 years earlier. One might note also that the foot crossing of the line has been removed. No 313017 departs for Richmond. *Author (2)*

ACTON CENTRAL

Then: 10 May 1978
The level crossing is still protected by semaphores worked from the adjacent box, but platforms have already been reduced to three car lengths only. A train for Broad Street formed of a Class 501 unit is departing.

Now: 27 October 1998
The crossing is protected by remotely controlled full barriers, the third rail electrification has been removed, and 25kV ac installed in its place.
No 313017 is proceeding towards North Woolwich. Acton Central is one of the changeover points at which pantographs are raised (eastbound) or lowered (westbound) and shoegear withdrawn or substituted.
Author (2)

WILLESDEN JUNCTION HIGH LEVEL

Then: December 1960
A locomotive with Great Northern origins, 'J50/3' 0-6-0T No 68961, has a respectable load for a trip freight as it heads east through the station platform.

Now: 27 October 1998
The use of three-car units only has resulted in the platforms being cut back to the shelter, and they no longer cross the dc lines below. This picture of No 313014 arriving with a North Woolwich train is thus the nearest that the 1960 picture can be reproduced. *John C. Baker/Author*

HAMPSTEAD HEATH

Then: 22 March 1973
A mixed consist rattles along behind Class 25/2 No 7528 as it emerges from Hampstead Heath Tunnel and hurries through the station.

Now: 8 December 1998
The station has been rebuilt, again. The long awnings which feature in the 1973 photograph and date from the 1950s extended the length of the wall on the right. What is there today, on both platforms, is of more recent construction. No 313102 brings in the 14.26 to North Woolwich. Only the houses above the footbridge provide a real link with the past.
Peter Dobson/Author

CAMDEN ROAD

Then: 21 July 1980
Despite two systems of electrification at this point, what was then the Camden Road-North Woolwich service required the use of diesel units. A terminating Class 105 Cravens twin has run forward and is about to cross over and return via the platform immediately to the left of the photographer. It can then take up its next working to North Woolwich.

GOSPEL OAK

Then: Undated, c1958

This picture shows one of the Class 15 BTH Type 1 800hp locomotives ('D82xx' number series) heading east with a freight on the approaches to Gospel Oak station. The locomotive was allocated to Devons Road, Bow. Before 1970, the North London passenger services had fourth rail electrification.

Now: 7 November 1998

The signalbox was destroyed by fire and replaced with the utilitarian structure in the background, colour lights supplant semaphores, platforms have been shortened, and a new platform with siding has been constructed for Tottenham & Hampstead services to Barking. This latter is behind the fence on the right-hand side. The picture was taken in the gathering gloom of a Saturday winter evening, in which engineering works had delayed the next eastbound service to beyond the hours of darkness. *Author's Collection/Author*

Now: 8 December 1998

The freight tracks to the right have been lifted, but two electrification systems remain, as does the box. Approaching from the Primrose Hill direction is No 37116, an EWS locomotive with a train of flat wagons. *Author (2)*

CALEDONIAN ROAD & BARNSBURY

Then: 21 July 1980
The departing DMU is heading west for Camden Road, and not as indicated. There are still four tracks through the station, which now has its entrance via the ticket office on the left; this view was taken from the station footbridge.

Now: 8 December 1998
No 313014 is leaving for Richmond, now an electric service from North Woolwich. The ticket office has been destroyed, but maybe the Way Out sign survived. The goods lines on the right have been electrified at 25kV ac, but become single-track from here (Barnsbury Junction) through to Canonbury, a mile away. There has been a general growth of vegetation.
Author (2)

HACKNEY WICK

Then: 21 July 1980
The DMU service from Camden Road arrives at the pristine station, two months after its opening.

CALEDONIAN ROAD & BARNSBURY

Then: Undated, c1925

This picture seems likely to have been taken after all electrification work (for the time being!) was completed, and hence around this period. This is the view looking east towards Roman Way, which crosses the railway in the distance and is clearly the main, if not the only, entrance to the platforms. Notably, platforms were provided on all four tracks.

Now: 8 December 1998

All the buildings in the 'Then' picture have gone, save only those on the bridge to the right. The station is now two basic platforms only, and there is no access to or from Roman Way. It is also severely vandalised. *Author's Collection/Author*

Now: 8 December 1998

A Freightliner service with No 90144 as the motive power hurries eastwards. In the years in between, the line has had both third rail and overhead electrification applied. *Author (2)*

HACKNEY WICK

Then: 21 July 1980
Eastbound and westbound services, both Cravens units, pass. This is the view looking east towards Stratford. Sir Peter Parker, then Chairman of the British Railways Board, was asked at the station's opening if there was anything particularly modern about it. 'Yes, it has no loos.'

Now: 8 December 1998
Silverlink Metro's No 313103 is departing for North Woolwich. Alas, today the station's buildings are all boarded up, the concrete footbridge has suffered major damage, and the whole has a general air of neglect.
Author (2)

KENSINGTON OLYMPIA

Then: 4 June 1980
The service for which this station is perhaps best known is the twice daily working from Clapham Junction, which was operated for Post Office employees. Various motive power was used over the years, here seen as Class 33 No 33042 and two MkI coaches. The locomotive has run round and is ready for the second return morning journey from Platform 2. Note that it will run as a Class 5 empty stock service.

Now: 14 December 1998
The half-hourly services of Silverlink between Clapham Junction and Willesden Junction require two Class 313 units for their provision. No 313014 on the left in Platform 2, with a District Line train behind (Platform 1), is departing for Willesden. On the right is the Clapham Junction service with No 313009 in Platform 3. The near platform has been moved further west and there is now no loop on this side. On the other hand, all lines are now bi-directionally signalled. *Author (2)*

KENSINGTON OLYMPIA

Then: 6 August 1969
Class 15 No D8201 arrives with the milk tank empties from Broad Street via Willesden Junction. In those days, there were four tracks between the two platforms.

Now: 14 December 1998
A lone Class 58, No 58036, follows along the same track as the Class 15; a comparison of the houses suggests that the locomotive is about level with the former foot crossing. The old platform ramp is still in place, but the signals are now colour lights. All lines are electrified on the third rail system.
J. H. Cooper Smith/Author

KENSINGTON OLYMPIA

Then: 4 June 1980
Class 25 No 25154 is in the process of running round the Motorail train standing in Platform 2, which it has brought in with sister locomotive No 25189. This will enable it to position the car-carrying wagons for loading in the terminal alongside (see below and overleaf).

Then: Undated, *c*1975
Cartic 4s (car-carrying, articulated sets of four wagons) being loaded for Perth.

Now: 14 December 1998
Connex SouthCentral No 319009 arrives in No 2 platform with the 09.37 Gatwick Airport to Rugby. The fine semaphore gantry has now been removed and third rail is in place.
Author/Author's Collection/Author

KENSINGTON OLYMPIA

Then: Undated, c1965
Motorail was intended to be big business, but it never quite took off. This posed publicity photograph shows the eager motorist and his family about to take the plunge.

Now: 14 December 1998
The same building now caters for more earthy needs, and is nothing to do with the railway. The loading platforms which were out of sight behind the frontage have been filled in. *Author's Collection/Author*

CLAPHAM JUNCTION

Then: 23 May 1995
This, the most recent 'Then' picture in the book, gains its inclusion by representing the fast vanishing traditional DMU on a duty where electrics have taken over — twice. This had already happened for the service to Kensington Olympia only, but service extension to Willesden Junction required DMUs to be reintroduced for a time. No 117701 forms the 08.33 departure.

Now: 8 August 1998
Silverlink Metro unit No 313121 in new livery and refurbished internally will be the 12.57 service to Willesden Junction. The grass on the track is beginning to grow. *Author (2)*

The Great Central Railway

Last main line into London, and also the first out; that is the mixed claim of the Great Central Railway. Reaching Marylebone in 1899, passenger services north of Aylesbury finally came to an end in 1966. Today, Marylebone's truncated four-platformed terminus has two outer suburban functions, serving as it does the line to Aylesbury and that via Northolt Junction to Banbury. There is a branch from Princes Risborough to Aylesbury, though operation is mainly provided by through services from Marylebone.

Services are all provided by Chiltern Railway Co, with 2tph from Marylebone to Amersham and Aylesbury. There are also 1tph to Birmingham Snow Hill, 1tph to Banbury, 1tph to Aylesbury via Princes Risborough and 1tph to High Wycombe.

The Great Central main line runs parallel with London Underground from Canfield Place, Finchley Road. Between Harrow-on-the-Hill and Amersham, Chiltern Railway operates over lines nowadays owned by London Underground and used also by the Metropolitan main line services from Baker Street. This was formerly the Met/GC Joint Line. Railtrack metals are rejoined at Mantles Wood, a mile or so to the north of Amersham.

Other Underground involvement is in the South to West Ruislip section, where the GC parallels that branch of the Central Line.

From Marylebone, the long St John's Wood Tunnel (1,606yd) is followed by Hampstead Tunnel (694yd). After this, there are just a few short tunnels, and the miniscule 80yd Saunderton Tunnel; this latter is on the up line only, the result of up and down line separation over the section between Saunderton and Princes Risborough. This is former GW/GC Joint territory, such are the problems of a latecomer to the scene.

Chiltern Railway also operates a residual service from Paddington over the otherwise unserved London end of the former Great Western's Birmingham main line. This is a much more direct route from Paddington than that via Reading.

The lines served by Chiltern underwent complete modernisation in the early 1990s, from the infrastructure through to the trains; this is a well-to-do market, and the traffic results have been encouraging. Attention has been given also to auxiliary services, such as car parking and security.

Recent infrastructure work has seen the doubling of the previously singled Princes Risborough to Bicester North section, and a second through platform is now once again provided at Princes Risborough. This is a railway which has seen its infrastructure cut to the bone; short of Banbury (69 miles) on the line via High Wycombe, the opportunities for faster trains to overtake others are very limited indeed. This imposes its own limitations on the services which can be offered.

If it comes about, the CrossRail project will absorb the whole of the Aylesbury via Amersham service, and Marylebone would be left to serve only the High Wycombe line. The station would look very empty with only four trains using it in an off-peak hour. One possibility perhaps is an upgraded service for the local stations nearer London. A rerun of the 1970s debate in which conversion to busway was proposed seems less likely nowadays to fit the political agenda.

MARYLEBONE

Then: 24 April 1981
The three separate roofed sections of the terminus are plain to see in this view from Rossmore Road, which passes above the platform ends. A four-car Class 115 set in a mixture of liveries — was there ever a better reminder that these were individual vehicles and not treated as sets? — runs into the terminus from Aylesbury.

Now: 17 December 1998
The furthest right section of the roof has gone, but attention to detail has meant that the canopy which was on the right of the demolished shed has been transferred across to the surviving former middle section. No 168003/04 may be seen to the left and right, while there are also a number of 165/0 units to be seen.
Author (2)

MARYLEBONE

Then: 12 May 1956
An 'Ian Allan Trains Illustrated' excursion prepares to leave behind ex-works 'A4' Pacific No 60014 *Silver Link*. This was the 'Pennine Pullman', a 10-coach train of which all but two were Pullmans. It was brought up at the rear with an Observation Car.

Now: 12 November 1998
Class 168 set No 168004 is stabled, approximately, on the site of the Pullman of over 40 years previously. This, the west side of the station, has been largely demolished, and both photographs were taken from the same island platform.
G. S. Robinson/Author

MARYLEBONE

Then: 5 July 1984
The Class 115 units had a substantial facility outside Marylebone, seen here from the west side and with the running lines in the foreground. The terminus is just out of the picture to the right.

Now: 17 December 1998
The yard has completely gone, including even the curved access road from street to platform level which can be seen in the 'Then' picture. The land has been sold for housing. No 168003 is moving away from the camera, bound for the platforms after a visit to the carriage washer. The washer is situated close to the boundary fence, but behind the photographer.
Author (2)

WEMBLEY STADIUM

Then: 5 July 1984
Nine minutes is a good timing for the 6.5 miles from central London to Wembley, but few people not in the know utilise the route for Wembley events. A basic 2tph service is not very attention grabbing, and how many have even heard of Marylebone station? An up Class 115 service for Marylebone arrives, catering mainly it would seem for schools traffic.

Now: 12 November 1998
No 165018 finds even less traffic, but to be fair this was the 12.53 from Banbury to Marylebone, a train which does not stop! As usual, the bushes have grown enormously. The station has also been relit. *Author (2)*

WEST RUISLIP

Then: 19 March 1982
A service departs for Banbury, having previously occupied the platform line. The two foreground sidings are the very ends of the Central Line tracks, pointing hopefully towards Denham for an extension which is unlikely ever to come. The line on the left provides rail access to the LUL Ruislip depot.

Now: 12 November 1998
No 168002 passes with the 12.53 Marylebone to High Wycombe. As the loop has been removed and the platform extended, some track rearrangements have been needed. The semaphores are also all now colour lights. *Author (2)*

PRINCES RISBOROUGH

Then: April 1948
This view was taken looking north; the approaching express freight train has LNER 'K3/2' 2-6-0 No 61913 in charge. On the left is GWR 2-6-2T '6100' class No 6108, shunting in the down platform. The latter is in GWR livery, unlike the 'K3/2' which has acquired BR numbers.

HIGH WYCOMBE

Then: 11 March 1961
The Great Central had varying affiliations with the BR Regions, and some suggested that this may have accentuated its downfall. The Sheffield end was always firmly part of the Eastern Region, and ex-LNER power was thus a regular feature. Class V2 2-6-2 No 60890 is in charge of a Women's Hockey Special from Rugby to Wembley as it passes.

Now: 12 November 1998
The tracks have been reduced from three to two, but the bridge still stands as do the houses. No 165009 is arriving as the 10.48 Princes Risborough to Marylebone.
H. K. Harman/Author

Now: 12 November 1998
Chiltern Railways is putting the down platform back into use, which work requires Railtrack to extend it across the site of the former loop. The other need is the reinstatement of a footbridge and all this work can be seen under-way in this picture. In the platform is the 09.50 Birmingham Snow Hill to Marylebone.
H. K. Harman/ Author

AYLESBURY

Then: 23 August 1950
The western side of Aylesbury station has always been used by the GWR branch trains from Princes Risborough and its successors. This is the 14.30 arrival at today's Platform 1, consisting of a GC Class N5/2 0-6-2T, No 69259, and two coaches. The archetypal GWR branch service it is not!

Now: 11 April 1998
Platform 3 on the former up main line sees the arrival of No 165031 with a terminating service, the 08.57 from Marylebone. This is the preferred platform, as it does not require the use of the footbridge for passenger access. The locomotive sheds on the right have become faceless office buildings. *E. C. Griffiths/Author*

AYLESBURY

Then: 23 June 1958
Class L1 2-6-4T No 67767 is in charge of the 1920 Quainton Road to Marylebone service, a six-vehicle consist which appears to include two articulated pairs. There is still an additional platform on the right and an active yard beyond.

Now: 3 October 1992
Dusk falls, and the train is a rather more modestly proportioned 18.15 to Marylebone, formed of No 165018. Rather less platform space is used, but the overall scene is similar.
M. Mitchell/Author

AMERSHAM

Then: Undated, *c*1958
The pre-electrification Amersham was no more than an intermediate stopping point for Metropolitan trains north of Rickmansworth. No 42251 is an ex-LMS Class 4 2-6-4T, seen here arriving with an up service of Metropolitan stock.

Now: 14 November 1998
The bicycle shed facility is still there and fourth rail electrification is in place. A turnback siding for Metropolitan trains has been installed, and an A stock train can just be seen, waiting for the approaching Chiltern Railways No 165036 to clear. The latter is the 09.08 Aylesbury to Marylebone.
Ian Allan Library/Author

CHALFONT & LATIMER

Then: 12 September 1960

This was the first day of electric services to Amersham and Chesham. A train formed of T stock enters the Chesham bay, a move which has been repeated twice an hour, except when through services are provided, ever since.

Now: 11 April 1998

The train is now A stock, and in this picture it is departing for Chesham. The branch junction has been simplified to single leads, and the goods yard is now a car park. Otherwise, business continues as normal. *J. P. Mullett/Author*

CHORLEY WOOD

Then: 15 June 1962

A train of T stock calls while working the 1959 Amersham to Rickmansworth, at that time one of the few T trains to be seen on the newly electrified section. This is car No 2729.

CHESHAM

Then: Undated, *c*1955
The Ashbury set of three vehicles is being hauled out of the station by ex-GC Class C13 4-4-2T No 67420. A run-round loop is provided.

Now: 13 April 1998
The overall scene is much the same, though the loop has been removed and the bay platform, put in at the time of electrification, has also now gone. An A stock train provides the service, leaving for Chalfont & Latimer. *Ian Allan Library/Author*

Now: 11 April 1998
This is a general view of the station as a whole, looking towards London. An A stock train for Amersham is approaching, and the distinctive canopies can be seen. The whole is most attractive. *L. Sandler/Author*

RICKMANSWORTH

Then: 19 September 1982
Metropolitan No 12 *Sarah Siddons* coasts through Rickmansworth on the up line with a special consisting of BR air-conditioned coaching stock. The tightness of the curves here is very evident, and this causes problems in the gaps which open up between rail vehicles and the platform.

Now: 14 November 1998
A Baker Street-bound A stock train arrives. Television screens are now in place to enable drivers to see back along the length of the train, and the canopies would seem to have undergone a substantial repair programme. Somewhat to the photographer's surprise, he was able to catch this train after a quick sprint through the subway. *Author (2)*

RICKMANSWORTH

Then: 6 November 1965
The bridge south of the station has long been used for an overall view of what is going on. Ex-LMS Stanier 'Black 5' 4-6-0 No 4514 passes through with the 08.15 Nottingham Victoria-Marylebone.

Now: 14 November 1998
The view is now restricted due to the bridge being encased in close mesh wire. There are no trains from Nottingham nowadays, but the now venerable A stock provides a basic 4tph service. An up service leaves for Baker Street. *M. J. Fox/Author*

RICKMANSWORTH

Then: 23 February 1952
A pair of Metrovick electric locomotives, No 18 *Michael Faraday* and No 7 *Edmund Burke*, stand in the sidings south of the station until they are required to take over a steam-hauled service arriving from Aylesbury.

Now: 14 November 1998
The goods shed and sidings have gone, to be replaced with a large car park. This is a Saturday, when usage is very limited. An Amersham to Baker Street train of A stock heads away south. *C. R. L. Coles/Author*

WATFORD

Then: 20 April 1977
South of the station, the Metropolitan Line crosses the Grand Union Canal on an impressive bridge. There is, however, no activity apart from the train of A stock for Baker Street, and there is no noticeable patronage on board the train either.

Now: 18 April 1998
In this view, a higher viewpoint has been used, and the locks in the background are visible. LUL corporate livery has the ability to 'lift' most pictures, especially when taken in less picturesque circumstances than this. *Author (2)*

NORTHWOOD

Then: July 1961
This is the view south from the station on the original alignment. Construction work on the left will introduce two new lines and a new station, those in the foreground becoming the fast lines and devoid of platforms.

Now: 14 November 1998
This signalbox has gone and a car park for the local supermarket now extends to the edge of the tracks. Chiltern Railways No 168005 is operating the 13.08 Aylesbury to Marylebone. *G M. Kichenside/Author*

PRESTON ROAD

Then: 1982
The antique lighting gives this view a certain period flavour, while the flats across the railway are also clearly not of recent construction. The modern touch is provided by the northbound A stock train for Uxbridge, but even this was in days before graffiti was a problem.

HARROW-ON-THE-HILL

Then: Undated, c1955
A train of T stock is seen on a southbound working in Platform 5. The station buildings look decidedly on the scruffy side.

Now: 14 November 1998
The station now appears considerably brighter, while commercial development has clearly taken place in the town centre. The A stock train will call at all Met stations to Baker Street. *Ian Allan Library/Author*

Now: 14 November 1998
The northbound A stock service is on the fast line. For some reason, the permanent way have placed plastic bags full of ballast at the side of the track. The station has been spruced up considerably, and the gardens are in trim. Lighting has been renewed, but the CCTV camera supports do not add to the overall effect. *Author (2)*

CANONS PARK

Then: April 1986.
The then almost new 1983 stock train is arriving, before all the passengers from the previous service have had a chance to leave the platform. This station is a good basic design, befitting its opening date of 10 December 1932.

Now: 14 November 1998
The lighting has been changed to a less intrusive variety and the 1983 stock has given way to the 1996 stock trains. Otherwise, matters remain much the same. *Author (2)*

NEASDEN DEPOT

Then: 16 January 1982
A light dusting of snow is a useful artistic addition to an otherwise drab scene, in which a 1972 MkII stock train is seen leaving the depot at the south end. The foreground tracks are those of the Metropolitan and Jubilee Lines.

Now: 8 December 1998
Some new buildings have been completed, and the track layout has been altered. In this view, a four-car A stock train is being shunted. The inner end seen here, without a red front, looks decidedly odd.
Les Bertram/Author

NEASDEN

Then: August 1956
This view from the North Circular Road bridge looking south shows the Metropolitan station with four platforms, albeit that only the centre island is in regular use (for the Jubilee Line). Metrovick Bo-Bo locomotive No 12 *Sarah Siddons* has a train for Aylesbury, while on the right the Great Central lines for Marylebone pass well clear of the station buildings.

Now: 8 December 1998
Some station reconstruction is evident, as are layout changes to the track. An A stock train for Amersham is overtaking a 1996 stock service.
R. M. Newland/Author

WILLESDEN GREEN

Then: 21 August 1985
A 1983 stock Jubilee Line train accelerates away as it leaves Willesden Green station on a southbound working to Charing Cross. The six-track formation includes two Railtrack lines left, the northbound Metropolitan, northbound and southbound Jubilee, and southbound Met.

Now: 8 December 1998
The station building has almost the look of a cardboard cut out perched on the station bridge, but the photographer can assure readers that it is genuine. On the left a Chiltern Railways Class 165 approaches, a northbound 1996 stock train can just be seen leaving the station, and in the foreground another is departing for Charing Cross. *Colin Boocock/Author*

BAKER STREET

Then: Undated, *c*1958
The Metropolitan's electric services and their steam-hauled extensions had remained unchanged for decades. The Amersham electrification itself would have been completed 15 or 20 years earlier had it not been for World War 2. In this timeless view, Metrovick No 12 *Sarah Siddons* is awaiting departure with a train for Aylesbury.

WEST HAMPSTEAD

Then: 8 February 1983
1972 MkII stock forms a southbound Jubilee Line working as it approaches the station. In the centre of the picture is a turnback siding, whose pointwork it will be noted is set for neither direction. As such, it provides a sort of double catch point, preventing any unauthorised movement from the siding from fouling the running lines. In the background, a northbound A stock Metropolitan train is about to cross the bridge over the North London line below.

Now: 16 October 1998
An A stock train bound for Aldgate drops down the bank towards the station, which is the other side of the road bridge. The Jubilee Line turnback seems to have had a high security fence placed around it, but other change is minimal. *Author (2)*

Now: 19 December 1998
Today, it is an A stock train arriving from Aldgate in Platform 2, and the ultimate destination is Amersham. There are a few small changes such as that to the girder spanning the tracks, but they are minimal.
Ian Allan Library/Author

The Great Western Railway

Paddington is firmly established as the London terminus of the Great Western Railway (GWR), although had things worked out differently GWR trains might well have terminated at Euston. The LNWR and GWR lines are very close to each other in the Old Oak Common/Kensal Green area.

Paddington it was to be, however. A station on the Bishop's Road site was opened in 1838. The present station dates from 1854, though it was subsequently extended. Served by Brunel's broad gauge trains, this was part of the distinctiveness of the GWR, much loved by later writers and commentators. The broad gauge finally came to an end in 1892, but it was only very recently that, horror of horrors, the paraphernalia of overhead electrification could at last be seen within those hallowed portals.

This was part of the work needed to establish the Heathrow Express service. Incidentally, rumours that the Class 332 Heathrow Express units would have cast numberplates and be given names such as Heathrow Castle, Southall Grange, and King Paddington turned out to be false.

The main line is four-tracked throughout to Didcot. The main lines are paired and on the south side, and the relief lines on the north. All the intermediate stations have platforms on the relief lines, but many have them on the main lines as well. There are junctions to the Birmingham line and with the North London line in the Acton area, and a whole series of passenger branches. In order, the traditional ones in the area covered are West Ealing (7 miles) to Greenford (which also forms a diversionary route); Slough (18 miles) to Windsor & Eton Central; and Maidenhead (24 miles) to Marlow. The latest addition, that to Heathrow CTA and T4, opened in 1998.

Parts of the goods branches to Brentford Dock and to Staines West survive, while there are considerable volumes of freight, especially in the construction, automotive and petroleum sectors.

Today, 18 trains leave Paddington in a standard off-peak hour, as follows:

- 1tph   South Wales   Great Western Trains
- 2tph   Bristol   Great Western Trains
- 1tph   West of England   Great Western Trains
- 6tph   Reading and beyond   Thames Trains
- 2tph   Slough   Thames Trains
- 2tph   Greenford   Thames Trains
- 4tph   Heathrow   Heathrow Express

Additionally, Virgin Trains offers an occasional service on CrossCountry from Paddington to destinations beyond Birmingham.

Electric services are confined to those of Heathrow Express, and the 25kV ac electrification of the main line does not extend beyond Airport Junction. There are no tunnels at any point in the London area, other than on the new line leading into Heathrow Airport.

London Underground occupies the northeast side of the station with its Hammersmith & City services, which dive under the main line and then leave it for Hammersmith in the Westbourne Park area. LUL services reappear at Ealing Broadway, where both the District and Central Line branches terminate. At Greenford, the Great Western line terminates in the central bay of the Central Line's island platform.

Like the Great Eastern, the line out of Paddington depends on CrossRail for the future of its suburban services. This will entail the electrification of the line to Reading and, presumably though not necessarily, the passenger branches.

The railway into Heathrow is an additional complication. If Terminal 5 goes ahead, a branch of Heathrow Express from Heathrow Terminals 1,2,3 will be constructed, and there are further possibilities beyond that. All schemes involving Heathrow require electrification of the services which enter the airport stations.

It may be added that BAA is presently involved in the promotion of a second service from Heathrow. This is intended to run to St Pancras, with intermediate calls at Hayes & Harlington, Ealing Broadway and West Hampstead.

PADDINGTON

Then: 24 November 1981.
Platform 1 is not the place where one might expect to find an experimental four-wheeled railbus, but No R3 (RDB977020) was resident at lunchtime on that day for BRB inspection. It was then being used experimentally on the Severn Beach branch. It can now be seen in the excellent Transport Museum at Cultra, Northern Ireland. Behind the railbus is No 47500 and train, having arrived with the 08.22 from Liverpool Lime Street.

Now: 5 November 1998
No 47851 has brought in the stock for Virgin CrossCountry's 09.06 departure for Manchester Piccadilly, very much an everyday occurrence.
Jeremy de Souza/Author

PADDINGTON

Then: Undated, *c*1958
In this night shot, 'Castle' class 4-6-0 No 7013 *Bristol Castle* is at rest in Platform 9 on the arrival side of Paddington.

Now: 5 November 1998
That same site is presently undergoing some rebuilding. Thames Trains' No 166218 is surrounded by scaffolding towers after arrival, although this is at 09.00.
D. Sellman/Author

PADDINGTON

Then: September 1967
The luxury Blue Pullmans had their colour schemes reversed in 1967, even if that deprived them of their popular names. Latterly, they plied between Paddington and Bristol or South Wales, with a mid day journey to Oxford and back. This provided work for four sets, with one set spare. The train is in Platform 4.

Now: 5 November 1998
Heathrow Express unit No 332005 is in Platform 6, with Great Western 125s occupying Platforms 4 and 5. The vantage point is the same, and the individual at the bottom of the steps has hardly moved in over 30 years! The 25kV wiring can hardly be detected. *Ian Allan Library/Author*

PADDINGTON

Then: 25 July 1946
This is the road exit from the cab rank which was then between Platforms 8 and 9. It emerges onto Praed Street at the side of the Great Western Hotel.

Now: 5 November 1998
The roadway is partially blocked with contractors' materials, but the setting is the same. However, the Chief Goods Manager no longer resides in the office on the left.
Ian Allan Library/Author

PADDINGTON

Then: January 1959
'Britannia' Pacific No 70029 *Shooting Star* approaches Platform 9 with the up 'Capitals United Express' from Cardiff General, which it left at 08.00 and was due into Paddington at 10.50. A fine array of searchlight signals adds interest to this view.

Now: 5 November 1998
The view from the same platform today is rather different, following large scale alterations in the intervening years. There is also the addition of overhead catenary. Thames Trains' No 166218 is arriving with the 08.41 from Reading.
Spencer Yeates/Author

PADDINGTON

Then: June 1965
A Class 52 Western diesel enters Paddington with the up 'Cornish Riviera', as seen across the layout from Platform 1.

Now: 5 November 1998
The huge Paddington goods building has gone and a two-car Class 165 unit takes its place amidst all the catenary. This view is from Platforms 2 and 3. *Anthony A. Vickers/Author*

ROYAL OAK

Then: March 1962
The 1949-built '15xx' 0-6-0PTs for heavy shunting work had a short wheelbase and also outside cylinders. Only 10 were built, and some could be found on empty coaching stock (ECS) workings into and out of Paddington. An unidentified '15xx' struggles past Royal Oak with a train of 12 bogies, bound for Old Oak Common.

Now: 17 December 1998
In clearer conditions, a pair of Class 332 Heathrow Express units leave Paddington on the down main line with the 14.55 departure for Heathrow. *Brian Haresnape/Author*

ACTON MAIN LINE

Then: 10 May 1978
Class 50 No 50030 *Repulse* brings an up West of England express along the relief line towards Paddington. The tracks of Acton yard stretch away into the distance, and employment of a Class 08 shunter was justified.

WESTBOURNE PARK

Then: 18 September 1979
With the A40(M) Westway dominating the background, No 50034 *Furious* hurries out of Paddington with a Plymouth-bound train. The diveunder carries the Hammersmith & City branch of the Metropolitan, replacing a flat crossing which was quickly deemed unsuitable.

Now: 17 December 1998
A Great Western InterCity set with power car No 43017 leading forms the 14.00 departure for Swansea. Principal changes are those associated with electrification, though as yet this benefits only four of the trains leaving Paddington each hour. *Author (2)*

Now: 5 November 1998
No 165114 passes the station which has now acquired some rather more upmarket bus shelters on the platforms, while the lighting has also been renewed. Platform indicators have been added, but as yet the information provided has its limitations. There are also mirrors for the use of drivers. The yard is only a shadow of its former self. *Author (2)*

EALING BROADWAY

Then: 14 June 1952
The Greenford service ran as a shuttle to and from Ealing Broadway. This was the operation, with 0-6-0PT No 5420 of 1931 with auto-trailer No W220W *Thrush*. The location is the up relief platform, with the trains of the Central Line behind.

Now: 5 November 1998
The shelter (which does not benefit Thames Trains' passengers) is intact, but the station entrance and the office block are of altogether more recent construction. No 165131 forms the 10.52 Greenford to Paddington service. *H. C. Casserley/Author*

WEST EALING

Then: 16 December 1962
In the days when Paddington served the West Midlands due to the limitations of the WCML in the course of modernisation, Class 52 No D1042 *Western Princess* takes the 14.10 Paddington to Birkenhead round the curve at West Ealing Junction to reach Greenford, due to engineering work on the (then) main Wycombe line.

WEST EALING

Then: 14 October 1989
A Freightliner train, thought to be a Southampton to Willesden working, passes West Ealing behind No 33101 on the up relief line. Use of the up relief is ideal for reaching the North London line in the Acton area.

Now: 5 November 1998
With the fast lines blocked due to an incident at West Ealing, all services were diverted via the up relief. The station is visible in the distance. A Great Western HST set makes the best time possible towards Paddington.
Alex Dasi-Sutton/Author

Now: 5 November 1998
No 166202 takes the up relief past West Ealing Junction. Signalbox, sidings and crossovers have all gone; the infrastructure at this location is now considerably more basic.
M. Pope/Author

DRAYTON GREEN

Then: 18 September 1979
No 31284 is in charge of a mixed freight heading towards Greenford, as a single unit diesel moves out of the station towards Ealing Broadway on the shuttle from Greenford.

Now: 5 November 1998
The station is looking sprucer and there is some new housing adjacent. No 60021 *Pen-y-Ghent* heads a train of aggregates through the station, though on this occasion it was not coincident with the local passenger service. *Author (2)*

SOUTHALL

Then: 18 October 1979
No 08944 is the well turned out Southall shunter, seen here at the eastern end of the station. The notice reads: 'Spring point, not to be operated unless authorisation given by Shunter or Traffic Assistant'. Authorisation is clearly being given.

GREENFORD

Then: 19 March 1982

The Class 121 Pressed Steel single unit No 55034 departs from Greenford for Ealing Broadway just slightly before the Central Line 1962 stock train. Lower quadrant semaphores are an increasing rarity, but those at Greenford are still in operation. This is certainly the nearest they get to Underground services.

Now: 19 December 1998

The 14.22 from Paddington arrives, formed of Thames Trains' No 165129. The lighting on this LUL-owned station has been replaced and so has the signalling for Underground trains. Otherwise, there is little change. *Author (2)*

Now: 5 November 1998

The distinctive footbridge is now encased. An up Great Western HST set, power car No 43124 at the rear, meets a Class 166 unit on the down relief line. *Author (2)*

SOUTHALL

Then: Undated, *c*1955
Ex-GWR '28xx' class 2-8-0 No 2894 heads a long mixed goods on the down relief as it approaches Southall. In the background on the right can be seen Southall shed, which includes a GWR railcar amongst the vehicles present. The extensive goods yards are seen on the left of the picture. The foreground includes an indication of the activity with an impressive display of rodding.

Now: 5 November 1998
Thames Trains' No 165114 on the down relief passes an automotive train on the up relief. None of the buildings on the left are now in railway use and the motive power depot is not part of the commercial railway. The effective boundaries are delineated by the area wired for 25kV.
Author's Collection/Author

SOUTHALL

Then: 18 September 1979
An up direction HST in full cry passes the well-known Southall landmarks at midday. It is of course in the then British Rail corporate livery, basically blue and grey. Power cars have a yellow cab roof and lower body sides, with the intermediate area black.

Now: 5 November 1998
The landmark buildings are unchanged, but 25kV has been added and BAA Heathrow Express train with No 332006 at its head is approaching on the up fast line. *Author (2)*

HAYES & HARLINGTON

Then: 18 September 1979
A Pressed Steel single unit No 55022 substitutes for a longer formation on a Slough-Paddington working. The train is on the up relief line.

Now: 6 November 1998
No 165106 provides a down line service on the relief lines. The GWR seats have been replaced by the NSE variety and there is new lighting, but all the buildings both on and off the railway are much as before. Electrification is the other change. *Author (2)*

SLOUGH

Then: 27 May 1963
Class 42 'Warship' No D812 *Royal Naval Reserve 1859-1959* passes on the down relief line with a fitted freight for the West of England. On the right, commercial vehicles are being loaded, and the central bay platform is being abolished.

IVER

Then: 11 March 1961
The single unit diesel is on a crew training run and presumably yet to enter service. It is on the up relief line and, of course, in the original smart livery. The track on the down fast line in the foreground almost has the appearance of model railway track, which has not been properly ballasted or weathered.

Now: 6 November 1998
Substantial vegetation growth made necessary a viewpoint as far across the bridge as this. No 58038 proceeds light engine on the down relief line towards Slough. The country atmosphere of the pictures is spoiled in real life by a constant stream of HGVs on the road just beyond the top of the embankment on the right.
M. Pope/Author

Now: 6 November 1998
Thames Trains' No 165121 leaves Slough with the 11.28 Paddington to Reading. A loading ramp is still available on the up side. All traces of the bay have gone, apart from a curious gap between the canopies for the two platforms. *P. J. Lynch/Author*

SLOUGH

Then: 25 September 1975
No 31257 is held in the up goods loop, awaiting a path onto the up relief. The buildings are still rail connected.

Now: 6 November 1998
An up Great Western HST approaches Slough. There are now no rail facilities for the factory areas, and some industrial redevelopment has taken place. *Author (2)*

SLOUGH

Then: 24 January 1979
The Slough-Windsor service has nearly always operated on a self-contained basis, if for no other reason than it would otherwise have to encroach onto fast line capacity. In the snow, Pressed Steel single unit No 55027 and trailer No 56287 (leading) depart with the 13.32 to Windsor & Eton Central.

Now: 6 November 1998
No 165003 is turned out by Thames Trains for today's services. This is the 12.02 departure. Railway space has been cut back to the passenger platform only, and the loading bay has become an access road to a car park on the far side of the bridge and behind the photographer. *Les Bertram/Author*

WINDSOR

Then: 2 May 1963
Viaducts stretch for 847yd on this, the Eton side of the Thames railway bridge, in the centre of the picture. Ex-LMS 'Jubilee' 4-6-0 No 45562 *Alberta* begins to lift a return excursion to Leeds up the bank to Slough.

Now: 6 November 1998
Today, the river bridge is almost hidden by trees, and the singling of the branch means that trains now use the track on the far side of the viaduct. And, as the branch is now no more than a long siding, there are no signals. No 165003 forms the 16.12 Slough to Windsor & Eton Central.
Gerald T. Robinson/Author

WINDSOR & ETON CENTRAL

Then: 21 May 1983
A pair of Class 121 power and trailer cars wait in the truncated facilities before returning to Slough.

Now: 6 November 1998
The station, albeit still named Central, has now been cut back so much that it is quite a long walk from the centre of the town. This is where a two-car unit, No 165003, now has to stand — way beyond the canopies. It makes one realise just how extensive the station once was, when it could absorb locomotive hauled excursions.
Author (2)

MAIDENHEAD

Then: 1 March 1979
Class 37 No 37257 backs a train of carflats into the Ford car depot from the up relief line.

Now: 6 November 1998
No 166220 calls at the same platform with the 12.35 Oxford to Paddington, in a scene that has witnessed little change.
Geoff Gillham/Author

MAIDENHEAD

Then: Undated, *c*1960
Ex-GWR '4500' class 2-6-2T No 5545 heads away from Maidenhead with a Taplow to High Wycombe unfitted freight train. The exemplary state of the formation, with cleared walkways, may be noted.

Then, later: 20 July 1978
Single unit and trailer Class 121 form the Marlow branch service, reversing at High Wycombe. The walkways are less well looked after, the embankments are becoming overgrown and the hut is now a pile of rubble.

Now: 6 November 1998
The 15.09 Marlow to Maidenhead is formed of No 165001, the embankments are on the way to being smothered, and would staff choose to walk by the side of the track now? Throughout this sequence, the distant view remains much the same.
Gerald T. Robinson/Author (2)

COOKHAM

Then: Undated, *c*1955
Cookham was then a two-platformed station used as a passing place on the single line, with a level crossing at the north end and a signalbox. A footbridge connected the platforms.

Now: 6 November 1998
The station has been reduced to a single platform and the level crossing has been converted to AOCL status (Automatic Open Crossing, Locally Monitored), but not much else remains. The 14.09 Marlow to Maidenhead calls. *Author's Collection/Author*

BOURNE END

Then: 7 July 1962
Ex-GWR '61xx' class 2-6-2T No 6143 on a Maidenhead to Aylesbury parcels train waits for the arrival of the 17.37 High Wycombe to Maidenhead DMU to clear the single line. The view was taken from the station footbridge.

BOURNE END

Then: 20 July 1978
The branch train arrives from Marlow, in what was once the down platform to High Wycombe but now comes to an abrupt end. Here the Class 121 power car and trailer will reverse, in order to reach Maidenhead. This entails train crew use of the ground frame on the right.

Now: 6 November 1998
The 13.42 Maidenhead to Marlow approaches; the procedure has not changed. The shelter on the near platform has gone. This platform is used only by peak services to and from Paddington, which run in conjunction with a Bourne End to Marlow shuttle. There has also been some commercial development on the site of what was once the Marlow branch bay platform. *Author (2)*

Now: 6 November 1998
The station building remains as it was, but everything beyond it — level crossing, signalbox, the lot — has gone. The platforms have been built up and a walkway created to allow access, and the removal of the footbridge. As can be seen, the railway line beyond is blocked by new development, even if there was not a road in the way. But Bourne End is still served, and so is the Marlow branch. *L. Sandler/Author*

The London & South Western Railway

The London & South Western Railway was the nearest to a 'proper' main line which could be found south of the Thames. The destinations it serves include Portsmouth, Southampton and Weymouth, and the latter-day watering places such as Bournemouth.

But it also served a large suburban network, nurtured by its General Manager Herbert Walker, who went on to occupy the same position in the grouped Southern Railway from 1923. In one word, this meant electrification. Electrification was coupled with the introduction of frequent clock-face timetables. Now they are commonplace, but they were an innovation then.

Today the main line from Waterloo, from west to east, comprises a line for Eurostar trains, three for Windsor line services, two for the fast main lines and two for the slow lines. The main lines become paired by direction between Earlsfield and Wimbledon through the use of a flyover.

After the West London line junction and others, Clapham Junction sees the divergence of the Windsor (and Reading) lines. As on the main line itself, which retains its four-track formation through to beyond Basingstoke (48 miles), there are many branches and indeed connecting links as well. Most of these are grade separated, though the most important junction at Woking (24 miles), for Guildford (30 miles) and Portsmouth, is a traditional flat arrangement.

Tunnels are noticeable by their absence, with short ones such as Chalk Tunnel (845yd) and St Catherine's (132yd) a little to the south of Guildford being the principal examples.

Service provision in the inner suburban area is based on a 2tph service, but more and more services combine as Waterloo is approached. Coupled with stops in longer distance services, this offers points such as Richmond 8tph, Surbiton 11tph and Epsom (via Wimbledon) 4tph. This refers to the midday off-peak period, and journey times do vary between trains.

All services in the area are provided by South West Trains, other than those of Eurostar and Wales & West. The inventiveness of the latter includes a Waterloo to Manchester via Newport service. There is a fringe involvement with Connex SouthCentral services, such as on the Epsom-Dorking corridor.

London Underground services may be found alongside at Wimbledon and Richmond, which are both District Line termini and, in the case of Richmond, that of Silverlink Metro as well. The other Wimbledon platforms, Nos 9 and 10, are used by Thameslink and (jointly) with Croydon Tramlink.

This is busy commuter territory, and electric multiple-units have long been predominant. A new build of electric stock is currently being delivered to South West Trains. Electrification is on the 750V dc third rail system. Diesel services are to be found at Waterloo; these are all those which proceed west of Basingstoke on the former West of England main line.

WATERLOO

Then: 6 June 1951
Luxury travel returns in the postwar era. The new 'Britannia' Pacific No 70009 *Alfred the Great* is preparing to depart with the principal train of the day for the Bournemouth line.

Now: 11 September 1998
For the last 10 years, the Bournemouth and Weymouth services have been dominated by the Class 442 Wessex Electric units. These have recently been repainted by South West Trains in the livery shown here and applied to No 2412. This is the 08.50 departure to Poole.
Author's Collection/Author

VAUXHALL

Then: 3 June 1967
Run-of-the-mill power for the Bournemouth line was the
Standard Class 5 4-6-0. No 73085 runs through Vauxhall on the
down fast line at about 08.00 with an unidentified train. This
was in the final weeks of steam working, as the general
condition of the locomotive suggests.

Now: 11 September 1998
Eurostar services are a recent addition; this is the 08.53 to Paris
Nord, the back end of which is only just leaving Waterloo. This
view is taken from further down the same platform, and
includes some well-known buildings in the distance.
Peter Ashton/Author

CLAPHAM JUNCTION

Then: 23 August 1976
Like them or not, the EPB units gave sterling service on the Southern's suburban lines for many years. Class 415/1 4EPB No 5127 arrives in Platform 10 with a service from Hampton Court.

Now: 12 November 1998
The platform canopies have been reduced considerably in their coverage, but seats and new lighting have been added on the near platform. No 455906 is approaching at the head of a contra-peak empty stock movement. *Author (2)*

CLAPHAM CUTTING, WEST

Then: 11 April 1978
Class 33 No 33008 is on the up fast line with a morning Salisbury to Waterloo working in snowy conditions.

CLAPHAM CUTTING, EAST

Then: 4 July 1967
Bulleid Pacific No 35028 *Clan Line* hurries through the cutting with the 08.35 Waterloo to Weymouth, shortly before all such steam operations became history. The train consists mainly, if not entirely, of Bulleid coaching stock.

Now: 1 September 1998
The appearance of the former Kent coast multiple-units on South Western metals and in Stagecoach SWT livery is still a cause of mild surprise. A working from Alton sees Fratton-based Class 411/5 No 1573 pass on the up fast line. The CEP units are now over 40 years old.
J. Scrace/Author

Now: 11 May 1997
All services are diverted to the up slow line and 4VEP unit No 3417 brings a Farnham to Waterloo working past a tamping machine on the up fast. *Author (2)*

SURBITON

Then: October 1946

This view of Surbiton station looking west from the Ewell Road bridge can still be seen today. 4SUB unit No 4163 is slowing to take the platform line from its position on the down fast. This was one of the earliest units, converted from steam stock by the LSWR from 1915 onwards, then rebuilt on longer underframes in the 1930s with bodies lengthened to increase seating capacity.

Now: 23 October 1998

The track layout is identical, although the crossover from the up slow to the up fast, partially obscured by the oncoming train, is clipped out of use. A six-car Class 159 formation forms the 12.40 Paignton to Waterloo, with unit No 159018 leading.
Author's Collection/Author

ESHER

Then: Undated, *c*1955

Class N15 4-6-0 No 30751 *Etarre* approaches Esher with an up express and passes the West signalbox.

SURBITON

Then: Undated, c1955
The use of a 'T9' 4-4-0 in suburbia was, let it be said, unusual. No 30310 is heading some form of special train as it pauses in the up fast platform with eight (or more) vehicles behind.

Now: 13 November 1998
No 158839 is a Wales & West Sprinter unit, seen here working the 15.17 Waterloo-Newport-Manchester Piccadilly. Free seat reservations are compulsory on all journeys east of Bath Spa. Physical change in this picture is confined to the platform lighting and the buildings outside the railway. *Author' Collection/Author*

Now: 25 October 1998
The west end of Esher station is now devoid of pointwork, and the whole area is controlled by colour lights. The 10.19 Alton to Waterloo is approaching on the up slow line, formed of South West Trains' No 423810.
Author's Collection/Author

WOKING

Then: Undated, *c*1960
The track area of the original Platform 1 at Woking was annexed for use as a bus terminating point in about 1970, and thus became part of the highway. This is where Bulleid Pacific No 35013 *Blue Funnel* is standing, facing towards London.

Now: 13 November 1998
The wall along the platform edge which resulted can be seen in this view, which includes a Class 442 unit departing for Waterloo. The houses are much the same, but there has been new development further away. Recent platform work, out of picture, has created a new terminating arrangement for trains from London. *Author's Collection/Author*

GUILDFORD

Then: April 1976
A Portsmouth Harbour to Waterloo semi-fast service emerges from Chalk Tunnel, immediately south of the station. The train is formed from 4CIG unit No 7340. The former motive power depot, from the area of which this photograph was taken, is now a car park.

GUILDFORD

Then: Undated, *c*1960
Ivatt Class 2 2-6-2T No 41287 stands in Platform 2 with a train for Horsham, via the long-closed branch through Cranleigh. The large Guildford station was never an appealing spot especially, as here, in the wet.

Now: 13 November 1998
This view is from the road bridge south of the station; Platform 2 has been rebuilt, with a new ticket office and station entrance alongside. Railtrack's No 930202 is a Fratton-based Sandite unit, used for seasonal leaf clearance. This is a conversion from the 1951 type 2EPB units.
A. G. Orchard/Author

Now: 13 November 1998
A track maintenance machine disappears into Chalk Tunnel; this is nowadays a highly mechanised activity. The surface car park has now become a multi-storey, and the railway land on the east side of the tracks has largely been cleared. *Author (2)*

70

MOTSPUR PARK

Then: 30 April 1984.
Class 423 4VEP No 7756 takes the place of the usual Class 455 units and offers Epsom to Waterloo passengers first class accommodation at standard class fares. This is an up Dorking to Waterloo evening service.

Now: 15 September 1998
The gasholders are still there, but empty, the signalbox has gone, and there are new buildings. No 455868 approaches at the front of a train from Epsom to Waterloo, as sister units leave. *Author (2)*

EWELL WEST

Then: 22 October 1980
Last of the Class 508 units for the
Southern, No 508043 arrives with an
Effingham Junction to Waterloo train.
On transfer to Merseyside, one trailer
remained on the Southern to be
incorporated into the 455/7 units
delivered in 1984/85.

Now: 16 September 1998
No 455871 is the lead unit arriving
with a service from Dorking to
Waterloo. The scene has changed
little; the low platforms are still in
evidence, and these can make
boarding and alighting from trains
quite difficult. *Author (2)*

EPSOM

Then: 22 October 1980
Cross-platform interchange between South Western and Brighton services has long been a feature of Epsom. No 508039 is on a Waterloo to Effingham Junction service, while Class 414/1 2HAP set No 5609 is at the front of a Victoria to Horsham duty. The signalbox always appeared to be a standard trackside model, but in an unusual location.

Now: 16 September 1998
No 455812 forms the 09.58 Dorking to Victoria service as it calls at Epsom's Platform 3. Without the box, the scene does look a little bare.
Author (2)

HAMPTON COURT

Then: Undated, *c*1930
Unit E20 was one of the 84 three-car units (as shown here) created from LSWR suburban steam stock. The torpedo ends made these trains distinctive. It would appear to be at the head of three similar units, making in all a nine-coach formation. This picture was taken from the signal box beyond the platform ends.

TOLWORTH

Then: May 1975
The prototype PEP units appeared in 1971 and were the preliminary designs for what became subsequently the Class 313/4/5 ac units and 507/8 dc units. Running as a pair of four-car units, Nos 4001 and 4002, they are seen here approaching Tolworth on the Chessington branch, with Tolworth Tower in the background.

Now: 15 November 1998
One of the ubiquitous Class 455 units is in the same position as it forms the 10.07 from Wimbledon to Chessington South. (The service was truncated due to engineering work.) Tree growth has altered considerably over the period. *Author (2)*

Now: 25 October 1998
There is now one island platform only, approached by two tracks with a scissors crossover between them. No 455841 will form the 10.09 departure for Waterloo. The land on the eastern side is no longer in railway use, but alternatives are limited by the crossing of the River Ember half-way down the platform. A bridge girder can just be detected in this picture. *Author's Collection/Author*

KINGSTON

Then: 27 October 1980
On a wintry morning, a train of Class 508 units bound for Waterloo crosses to the south side of the Thames, just as a 4SUB unit in plain blue livery disappears off picture to the left. In the foreground, the pleasure boats are tied up for the winter.

Now: 13 September 1998
A single Class 455 unit makes the same crossing. The riverside area has been cleaned up considerably, and the now redundant power station demolished. *Author (2)*

BARNES

Then: 1 March 1980
The ornate Barnes station building is remote from the passengers, as services are concentrated on the central island platform rather than the two side platforms. 4CIG No 7337 forms a down Waterloo to Reading service.

Now: 25 October 1998
No 455742 is providing a Staines via Richmond service. The station building is now in private ownership, but there is little change to its appearance. *Author (2)*

VIRGINIA WATER

Then: 23 September 1943
This view is towards Staines and London. The station fittings have had white paint applied as appropriate to make them visible in blackout conditions. Semaphore signals are controlled from the box on the platform, and the junction for Weybridge is beyond the station with that line diverging to the right.

Now: 13 November 1998
The station buildings have been replaced with a 1960s prefabricated system and work is in progress on repainting the footbridge. However, the signalbox has completely disappeared, and colour lights are in evidence. *Author's Collection/Author*

WINDSOR & ETON RIVERSIDE

Then: 23 August 1977
The 17.14 to Waterloo is an eight-car formation with 2SAP No 5905 (Class 418/1) leading. Windsor Castle can be seen in the background. The station then had three platforms.

ASCOT

Then: December 1938
This classic view of a train from Waterloo approaching Ascot station was taken immediately following the line's electrification that same year. As always, semaphore signals were retained, and a modest attempt at topiary has been made on the bush between the tracks. The leading unit is 2BIL No 2147, part of a six-car formation of similar units.

Now: 13 November 1998
The yard crane has gone and the area turned into a car park, and colour lights are in place, but the barrow crossing is still there 60 years later. Stagecoach-liveried 4CIG unit No 1320 is at the front of the 10.07 Waterloo to Reading as it approaches. The view is from Platform 3.
Author's Collection/Author

Now: 13 November 1998
No 455865 leaves Windsor with the 08.44 to Waterloo. Some of the space taken by the bay platform nearest the fence has been sold and developed for office use. The area out of camera to the right remains as a car park, and substantial foliage growth is under way. *Author (2)*

The London, Brighton & South Coast Railway

The Brighton company was a pioneer of suburban electrification, although the company decided that this was to be an overhead system at 6,700V ac. Work commenced with the Victoria-London Bridge service in 1909, and the system reached its greatest extent in 1925. By then, routes as far out as Coulsdon North and Sutton were electrified.

The inevitable retrenchment and conversion to third rail was undertaken in 1928-29 under Southern Railway auspices. But this was no more than a minor setback, and the major main line scheme to Brighton was completed in 1933. From Victoria, every hour, on the hour, in the hour was the Southern's justified boast. By the outbreak of war in 1939, all the former LBSCR lines of any importance had been treated similarly. This is essentially a suburban railway, with major traffics at locations such as Croydon, Norwood Junction, Redhill and Sutton. In more recent times, Gatwick Airport has gained considerably in importance.

The Brighton line has its city terminal at London Bridge, alongside the South Eastern station but fully integrated into it. This complements the West End terminal at Victoria of 1860. Victoria is two stations side by side, the other having been built by the London, Chatham & Dover Railway. The main lines from each Brighton terminus converge at Windmill Bridge Junction, to the north of East Croydon (10 miles). Each is four-tracked, but whereas the fast and slow Victoria lines are paired separately, those from the City are paired by direction.

The four-tracking continues, the fast and slow line routes separating for the tunnels through the North Downs; as a result, only the slow lines serve Redhill. Two tracks only are provided from Balcombe Tunnel (1,141yd) onwards.

There are a large number of other routes, not least within Greater London. There are, for instance, no less than three ways of reaching Sutton from the central London direction. There is also a supporting branch line network, still largely intact until the more rural parts of the territory are reached.

The main tunnels are associated with piercing the North Downs, as in Quarry Tunnel (1 mile 353yd), Merstham Tunnel (1 mile 71yd) and Oxted Tunnel (1 mile 501yd). The Oxted and Uckfield lines are particularly afflicted with tunnels, while further south the South Downs have to be contended with.

Today, three operators provide the majority of passenger services. Gatwick Express provides a 4tph nonstop service from Victoria to Gatwick Airport. Thameslink operates an 8tph service from the Midland main line north of the Thames. Of these 4tph proceed via London Bridge to Brighton, and the other 4tph provide, alternately, the clockwise and anticlockwise services around the Sutton/Wimbledon loop. All other services are provided by Connex SouthCentral, apart from minor incursions by Thames Trains (to Gatwick), by Virgin CrossCountry to Brighton and by Connex SouthEastern. Services are generally not less than 2tph and sometimes rather more, but where services are combined at key points or over sections which are served by more than one route, this is much enhanced.

The only time that Underground trains may be seen is at New Cross Gate, where the western branch of the East London Line terminates.

One loss to the Brighton (and parts of the South Eastern) networks for heavy rail came about as a result of the construction of Croydon Tramlink. Lines transferred include Wimbledon-West Croydon, Elmers End-Addiscombe, and Woodside-Sanderstead, though the latter had been closed rather earlier and only parts of it are being reused. Tramlink also parallels the Beckenham Junction spur from Birkbeck through to the terminus.

Further south, the railway suffered widespread closures from the 1950s onwards. East Grinstead (30 miles), once a four-way junction, is now only a terminus for the line from Croydon via Oxted. It was also, however, the northern end of the Bluebell Railway, today the first of the standard gauge preserved lines. While Bluebell trains have yet to reach East Grinstead, there is every hope that this will be achieved within the next few years.

Electric multiple-units provide nearly all the services other than for Gatwick Express, which is presently formed of a locomotive, trailer sets of coaches and a driving van trailer. Diesel units remain in use on the non-electrified Oxted-Uckfield service, and on the Thames Trains service from Reading via Redhill to Gatwick Airport. The few Virgin CrossCountry trains to Brighton are locomotive hauled.

The Thameslink 2000 scheme will treble the number of trains which can use the tunnel from King's Cross through to Blackfriars, and make related improvements to the line through London Bridge. Suitable destinations south of the Thames will have to be found for these services, and a substantial reorganisation of operations will be needed.

VICTORIA

Then: September 1975
Commuters stream off the trains at Platforms 9 and 10 in the morning peak period. These platforms serve the inner suburban area. On the left is 4SUB unit No 4639, a Class 405/2 of 1949 vintage.

VICTORIA

Then: 3 October 1977
4BIG unit no 7401 (Class 421/1)
heads a Littlehampton via Worthing
train out of the station.

Now: 19 December 1998
A VEP unit in Connex SouthCentral
livery leads the 10.02 Victoria to
Portsmouth Harbour/Bognor Regis
service away from the terminus.
Author (2)

Now: 1 September 1998
The whole area has been
comprehensively roofed over, with
retail developments above. The buffer
stops were also moved back and the
platforms shortened. Today's scene
thus bears little resemblance to that of
the 1970s. *Author (2)*

VICTORIA

Then: 23 August 1976
The 07.33 Uckfield to Victoria coasts down Grosvenor Bank to the terminus behind No 33019, with eight vehicles in tow.

Now: 19 December 1998
Class 455 units arrive at and depart from Victoria on the Brighton tracks to the west side of the formation. The scene is that of a busy and well-used railway. *Author (2)*

WANDSWORTH COMMON

Then: 26 March 1981
4SUB unit Nos 4743 and 4749 form the 14.49 Victoria to East Croydon as they approach Wandsworth Common on the down slow line.

CLAPHAM JUNCTION

Then: May 1981
Refurbished Class 415/1 4EPB unit
No 5405 leads its train into Platform
15 with a Victoria-Crystal Palace-
Selhurst working.

Now: 17 September 1997
No 455809 heads an Epsom Downs
via Norbury service into a station
which has changed little. A yellow line
has appeared near the platform edge
and a four-car unit with 392 seats unit
has been replaced by one with 316
seats. *Author (2)*

Now: 11 November 1998
No 455823 is on the 10.22 Victoria-
Crystal Palace-London Bridge service,
while an up Gatwick Express passes.
Les Bertram/Author

EAST CROYDON

Then: 15 September 1963
Caledonian Railway 4-2-2 No 123 and LSWR 'T9' 4-4-0 No 120 are together in charge of the 'Blue Belle' special as it halts at East Croydon.

Now: 14 September 1998
A Gatwick Express with No 73202 *Royal Observer Corps* propelling passes through Platform 2, which is nowadays a reversible line. Considerable station rebuilding has taken place in the interim, but the station is recognisably East Croydon. *Author's Collection/Author*

PURLEY OAKS

Then: 19 July 1959
The 6PUL/6PAN sets (the former with a single Pullman car, the other a pantry car) were introduced with the Brighton electrification of 1933. They were associated with this and the complementary services for nearly 40 years. 6PUL set No 3007 heads an Eastbourne-Victoria train through Purley Oaks on the up fast line.

Now: 16 September 1998
A Brighton-Victoria semi-fast service has Class 421/3 No 1736 at its head as it passes through a little-changed station. These fast platforms are not in general passenger use.
R. S. Carpenter/Author

NORTH OF STAR BRIDGE, COULSDON

Then: 28 May 1982
The visit of Pope John Paul II to Britain involved turning out a special train from Gatwick Airport to Victoria headed by No 73142 *Broadlands*. As will be seen the headcode used was HF, standing so it was said for Holy Father. All other journeys were made either by helicopter or by one of the purpose-built 'Popemobiles'.

Now: 16 September 1998
Also on the Quarry line, as opposed to the slow lines which are routed via Redhill, is No 47826 with one of the twice daily Virgin CrossCountry services from Brighton. This is the 14.15 Brighton to Preston. In each case, the Redhill line is at a lower level, to the bottom left. *Author (2)*

QUARRY TUNNEL, SOUTH END

Then: 27 August 1960
A Walsall-Hastings train headed by 'Schools' class 4-4-0
No 30900 *Eton* exits from Quarry Tunnel with 10 coaches. The
almost manicured appearance of the chalk cutting is noticeable.

Now: 16 September 1998
Today's photographer must go for a far more vertical shot, and
even then the line could be easily mistaken for being single.
Readers are assured, however, that this is the same location.
No 319220 is a Connex SouthCentral unit which has been
refurbished for the express services to Brighton. This is the
10.40 Victoria to Brighton. *Author's Collection/Author*

MERSTHAM

Then: 4 September 1979
Class 421/1 No 7304 is the leading vehicle of a Victoria-Horsham-Bognor Regis service, passing Merstham on the Redhill line. The Quarry line passes under the bridge behind the signalbox in the background. The CIG units were built for Brighton services. The three-letter description combined C for Corridor with IG, the telegraphic code for Brighton.

Now: 16 September 1998
No 319426 is a Thameslink train which is seen here working the 10.42 Bedford-Brighton. The signalbox and semaphores have gone, and the gash in the landscape at right angles to the railway, which contains the M25, has been largely obscured by vegetation growth. *Author (2)*

BALCOMBE

Then: 12 November 1980
A VEP unit approaches the station at speed on the down line, early on a frosty morning.

GATWICK AIRPORT

Then: 1959
This photograph was taken out of the window of a Victoria-Littlehampton train which, for some reason, was on the slow line and standing at Platform 2. This is the basic station as it was when it opened on 28 May 1958, seen looking northwards.

Now: 23 September 1998
From Platform 2, the baggage lift towers and footbridge can still be seen, though there is now no box. The line-up of trains from left to right are Connex SouthCentral Class 421/4 No 1834 on a Bognor Regis service, and Class 319 units of Thameslink and Connex SouthCentral respectively.
Author (2)

Now: 23 September 1998
The down platform has been shortened, ending at the point that the Thameslink Class 319's cab has reached. Both lines are bi-directionally signalled. Thameslink is the principal service provider at Balcombe.
Author (2)

LONDON BRIDGE

Then: 7 May 1980
The Brighton line platforms at the end of the morning peak see mostly EPB units, but also CIG unit No 7315 and VEP unit No 7752. Traffic falls during the midday lull, but the opening of the Jubilee Line in 1999 makes London Bridge a much more attractive interchange point for reaching the West End.

Now: 3 November 1998.
The station is quiet, interrupted by the arriving Class 456 two-car unit on the shuttle from Victoria, and a stationary Class 455 unit. Evidence of high rise construction can also be seen.
Author (2)

CRYSTAL PALACE

Then: Undated, c1950
4SUB unit No 4308 on a Victoria to Beckenham Junction service has just come to a stand. This was one of the 1925-built three-car sets, later augmented to four cars. Slight differences in the third vehicle can be detected. A signalbox is visible through the bridge.

Now: 11 November 1998
No 456009 is working the 10.59 London Bridge to Beckenham Junction and calls at Platform 2. The platforms beyond have been abandoned. However, much of the character of the station survives. *R. C. Riley/Author*

TADWORTH

Then: June 1977
The Tattenham Corner branch has never been a money-spinner. A down train from Charing Cross is formed of 2EPB unit No 5660, from which point onwards it is heading north towards London and also its terminus. The main station building on the road bridge was already in use for non-railway purposes.

Now: 16 September 1998
For EPB read Class 456 unit No 456005 and a service originating from London Bridge rather than Charing Cross. Twenty years on, the most noticeable change is the removal of the access slope on the down platform by the Way Out sign. Passengers now have to use an alternative route behind the boarded-up hut. *Author (2)*

SUTTON

Then: 1929
Railway building can result in substantial engineering works, the difficulties of which are increased in built-up areas. The Wimbledon & Sutton railway had to cross Grove Road, Sutton, while falling steeply to reach West Sutton station. This view shows the cutting under construction, Grove Road being that on which the house on the right stood.

TATTENHAM CORNER

Then: June 1977
Having three platforms, this was always a useful stabling point for EPB units. Seen here are Nos 5409 and 5418. This was one of those termini which was not short of room, even though it was only for Derby Day racecourse traffic in June that large crowds might be expected.

Now: 16 September 1998
The station buildings were demolished by a train overshooting the buffers some years ago, and rebuilding has been on a more modest scale. The two-car Class 456 unit looks lost amongst the wide open spaces. *Author (2)*

Now: 14 September 1998
The house is still there, separated from the double-track railway which is way below it by a substantial wall. *Author's Collection/Author*

WHYTELEAFE

Then: December 1977
A 4EPB unit arrives at Whyteleafe on a Caterham to Charing Cross service. This is still the traditional railway, with swing level crossing gates and semaphores.

Now: 16 September 1998
Lifting barriers have replaced the gates, and colour light signals the semaphores. The station car park has also been much extended. No 455801 is approaching with the 16.11 Caterham to London Bridge.
Author (2)

OXTED

Then: 7 May 1952
Wainwright 'H' class 0-4-4T No 31517 crosses Oxted Viaduct on a fine spring day. This view is thought to have been taken from Woodhurst Lane, west of the railway, with the train travelling north towards Oxted. Unfortunately, journey details are not recorded; Tunbridge Wells West was perhaps the most likely origin.

Now: 23 September 1998
Practicalities dictated the picture being taken from the east side of the line at the edge of the A25. The train is a 4VEP unit forming the 10.53 Victoria to East Grinstead. *Author's Collection/Author*

HEVER

Then: 26 April 1979
Class 207 Oxted unit No 1306 is
arriving on the down line with a
Victoria-Uckfield train. The platform
signalbox, a typical LBSCR feature, is
switched out of use, and the
semaphores are in the clear position.
Habitation anywhere near the station
is minimal.

Now: 23 September 1998
The 12.00 Uckfield to East Croydon is
seen departing, formed of unit
No 207202. The unstaffed station is in
immaculate condition, and basic
waiting shelters have made their
appearance. The signalbox has gone.
A helpful notice at the exit shows the
route to Hever Castle for the benefit
of visitors. The station building is now
private offices. *Author (2)*

ERIDGE

Then: 13 July 1981
By this stage, this was the only locomotive-hauled train, the 17.20 London Bridge to Uckfield. It is arriving at Eridge behind No 33024. All other services were operated with diesel units.

Now: 21 September 1998
The line has been singled, the remains of the down line being left in place for the possible future benefit of the Spa Valley Railway. No 205018 is arriving with the 12.48 East Croydon to Uckfield. *Author (2)*

ERIDGE

Then: 26 April 1979
Eridge was the terminus of the service from Tonbridge and Tunbridge Wells; this shunted to the bay platform (right). The train today is Class 207 unit No 1304. This provided connections to the Uckfield line and sister unit 1312 leaves with an Uckfield-Victoria service. This was a true country junction station.

Now: 21 September 1998
The growth of vegetation required the photographer to resort to the platform. The track in the bay (right) has been lifted; the train consists of unit No 205009 in Connex SouthCentral livery. This is the 13.00 Uckfield to Oxted. *Author (2)*

EAST GRINSTEAD

Then: Undated, *c*1957
Standard Class 4 2-6-4T No 80147, a Brighton design, is performing on the 'sulky service'. This was the minimal operation which British Railways were forced to introduce from 7 August 1956 between East Grinstead and Lewes as a result of the actions of Miss Bessemer of Chailey. The service ceased, finally for BR, on 17 March 1958. Part of the line now forms the Bluebell Railway.

Now: 23 September 1998
4VEP unit No 3437 is stabled in the same platform. The present footbridge between the two platforms replaces the original pedestrian route via East Grinstead High Level station. This crossed the Low Level station at right angles, but all traces of this have long since gone. *G. S. Robinson/Author*

SHEFFIELD PARK

Then: 23 April 1955
The 17.18 train from Brighton behind Standard tank No 80019 meets the 16.18(SO) service from London Bridge with No 80031 as motive power.

Now: 23 September 1998
LBSCR Class E4 0-6-2T No 473 *Birch Grove* backs down onto its Bluebell Railway train to Kingscote. It was BR No 32473. The small sign next to the semaphore on the left points out that it is on the line of the Greenwich meridian — something British Railways would have been most unlikely to do. Perhaps these pictures should be shown in reverse order, since 'Now' purports to be longer ago than 'Then'. *G. S. Robinson/Author*

TUNBRIDGE WELLS WEST

Then: 30 April 1984
Class 207 unit No 1308 emerges from the tunnel on the 13.52 Tonbridge to Eridge service. The signalman is waiting to pick up the token, and it will be seen that the points are set for the train to pass to his right-hand side.

Now: 21 September 1998
The closure of this line has resulted in the signalbox area being turned into a coach park. *Author (2)*

TUNBRIDGE WELLS WEST

Then: 30 April 1984
This was the view looking west from the road overbridge in the previous picture, showing the grand building which the Brighton company erected in a town which they must have considered to be a valuable source of traffic. Class 207 unit No 1308 forms the 12.34 Eridge to Tonbridge.

Now: 21 September 1998
New construction almost completely obstructs the 'Then' view of the station. This picture shows how the building itself has been extended and turned into a restaurant, and steps arranged from the platform to the car park.

More now: 21 September 1998
The locomotive shed on the far west side of the station is still intact and in use by the Spa Valley Railway. Its own station is alongside; the railway has not left Tunbridge Wells West.
Author (3)

The South Eastern & Chatham Railway

The Joint Committee which managed this amalgam of companies from 1899 was the operator of rail services in Kent and into London. The dual origins (formerly the South Eastern Railway and the London, Chatham & Dover Railway) resulted in its serving the termini at Charing Cross, Cannon Street, Blackfriars, Holborn Viaduct and Victoria.

Four-tracking on the South Eastern extends from Charing Cross/Cannon Street through London Bridge, to Chislehurst (11 miles) where large-scale construction of grade separated junctions as part of the Kent coast electrification scheme took place in the 1950s. Here, it is now possible to route trains to and from the Chatham lines which originate from Victoria. The South Eastern four-track section ends at Orpington, while the Chatham is four tracks only between Shortlands (10 miles) and Swanley (17 miles). However, the number of alternative routes available offers more flexibility than is at first apparent. On the Chatham, for instance, there is a route from Victoria to Shortlands via Catford as well as the main line via Sydenham Hill.

A key commuter area is contained in the three lines to Dartford (17 miles), via Woolwich, Bexleyheath and Sidcup respectively. On each of these, a 4tph service is usually provided. Again, service frequency in the area seldom falls below 2tph.

Major tunnels may be found at Penge (1 mile 381yd) and Sevenoaks (1 mile 1,693yd), though there are many others. On the Tonbridge-Hastings line, substandard clearances resulted in the provision of special stock for many years, though single-tracking the tunnels concerned has made this unnecessary now. Another problem is the limited distance between Wells and Grove Hill tunnels in which Tunbridge Wells station is positioned. This results in inadequate platform lengths for 12-car trains.

A further South Eastern route is that from Tonbridge via Redhill (where reversal is necessary) to Dorking, Guildford and Reading. The Reigate to Guildford and Ash to Wokingham sections are not electrified, and Thames Trains offers diesel multiple-unit services on this route west of Redhill.

Other operations are in the hands of Connex SouthEastern or occasionally Connex SouthCentral, apart from the brief incursion of Thameslink trains via Blackfriars, and the Eurostar services originating from Waterloo International. Third rail electrification is provided, and all services are operated by multiple-units.

London Underground's East London Line terminates at a bay in New Cross station.

Services in the area will need to be rethought when the Channel Tunnel Rail Link comes into operation; in the shorter term, South Eastern services may benefit from the Thameslink 2000 scheme.

VICTORIA

Then: Undated, c1955
'Britannia' Pacific No 70004 *William Shakespeare* was for several years the star turn on the 'Golden Arrow', a duty shared with No 70014 *Iron Duke*. They were kept suitably polished. To the right is 'West Country' Pacific No 34103 *Calstock*.

Now: 19 December 1998
Station remodelling requires a vantage point nearer the buffer stops. From left to right can be seen Class 423 No 3511, a Class 465, and a new Class 365 No 365512.
Author's Collection/Author

VICTORIA

Then: May 1967
Class 71 electric Bo-Bo locomotive No E5004 has arrived at Platform 2 with the Night Ferry train from Dover, which conveyed Wagons-Lits sleeping cars from Paris and Brussels.

Now: 19 December 1998
As elsewhere, the buffer stops have been set back. Most of the railway details are similar, though the terrazzo flooring certainly brightens the place up. No 365505 will form the 10.05 to Ramsgate, quite an improvement on the 4CEP units.
Brian Stephenson/Author

WANDSWORTH ROAD

Then: 13 May 1980
4CEP unit No 7191 passes the South London line station in the early morning haze with a train from Victoria to Margate.

Now: 11 November 1998
On a brilliantly clear afternoon, No 365516 hurries the 14.41 Victoria to Dover Priory past on the Kent lines. The signalling has been altered and Wandsworth Road station has gained a new footbridge. *Author (2)*

DENMARK HILL

Then: 13 May 1980
No 73138 is bound for Hither Green via Nunhead and Lewisham with a short train of steel coil.

Now: 11 November 1998
This view of the station area looking west shows the approach of dual voltage Class 92 No 92023 *Ravel* with a Channel Tunnel freight train from the West London line. The station buildings are only partly in railway use; the other part is a public house.
Author (2)

CHARING CROSS

Then: 21 April 1951
'Schools' Class 4-4-0 No 30912
Downside is ready to leave; on the
right is 4SUB unit No 4249 on a
service to Dartford.

Now: 21 September 1998
The old Charing Cross has been
surmounted by this new development
although the platforms are much the
same. Indeed, there is little room for
manoeuvre in what is at best a
minimum space city terminus. Short-
distance traffic is now the preserve of
the Class 465/466 units, though older
stock is still to be seen on the longer-
distance services (left). The Southern
Railway initials continue to hold the
two pictures together.
P. H. Wells/Author

CANNON STREET

Then: 5 April 1957
Light Pacific No 34076 *41 Squadron* is using the triangle of lines to turn, prior to making its return trip from Charing Cross. This was immediately following the fire which destroyed the signalbox, the remains of which can be seen at the foot of the left-hand station tower. The station is otherwise devoid of trains.

Now: 27 March 1992
The station roof has long been dismantled, but redevelopment leaving the towers in place is relatively recent. This is the new track layout as seen from an approaching inspection saloon; there are now seven platforms. *Author's Collection/Author*

GROVE PARK

Then: 25 March 1981
An empty 4EPB set, Class 415/1 No 5193 arrives at Grove Park from the Bromley North branch, having been stabled at the terminus during the day. It will proceed to Cannon Street to take up a down evening peak working.

Now: 21 September 1998
No 466005 is providing the services between Grove Park and Bromley North. There is now no connection from the down main line to the branch as seen in the 'Then' picture; such a move can only be made using the ladder of crossings on the London side of the station. On the other hand, the service is entirely self-contained, and there would seem to be no operational reason preventing the branch from being reduced to single-line siding status. *Author (2)*

PETTS WOOD

Then: 30 April 1984
The original EPB unit of Class 415/1, No 5001, is arriving with an Orpington to Cannon Street service on the up slow line. These were part of the massive postwar build for the Southern of similar trains; this unit dated from 1951.

ELMSTEAD WOODS

Then: 30 April 1984
Former Class 203 buffet car unit
No 1034, now reduced to five cars, is
on the up slow line and at the front of
the 15.40 Hastings to Cannon Street.

Now: 21 September 1998
The number of poles needed to
provide lighting and other services
seems to have increased alarmingly.
No 465202 can however still be
detected at the front of the 16.34
Orpington to Charing Cross.
Author (2)

Now: 21 September 1998
Years later, No 465009 leads a six-car
formation into the station, which has
changed little in the intervening time
apart from equipment for driver-only
operation. This is the 15.38 Orpington
to Charing Cross. *Author (2)*

SEVENOAKS

Then: 30 April 1984
Class 47 No 47486 takes its train through the curves at the south of Sevenoaks station with a return charter train to the London Midland Region. The apparent four-tracking quickly reduces to two for the long Sevenoaks tunnel about half a mile away. The EPB unit on the left is not on a running line, but stabled in a siding.

Now: 21 September 1998
Eurostar unit No 3211 is a French set running on the up main line, which will route it via Orpington. This is the 08.13 Paris Nord to London Waterloo International. Some layout changes may be seen, also some signalling alterations which increase the amount of bi-directional working. *Author (2)*

TONBRIDGE

Then: 13 July 1981
The Hastings line curves away to the right; that straight ahead is to Ashford. Class 207 unit No 1314 is shunting between platforms, while the Class 415/1 EPB set with No 5227 leading is stabled.

Now: 21 September 1998
Railtrack's Sandite vehicles are out in force, and the approaching No 930005 was once part of a 4SUB unit. As can be seen, the yard area has been cleared. *Author (2)*

HIGH BROOMS

Then: 16 October 1978
Class 207 unit No 1315 calls with a Tonbridge to Eridge local service. This was part of the non-electric railway.

Now: 21 September 1998
The 11.07 London Bridge to Tunbridge Wells via Redhill calls at High Brooms, the train made up with Class 423 VEP unit No 3582. This well-kept station has seen little change other than the addition of the third rail. *Author (2)*

NEW BECKENHAM

Then: 31 July 1978
2EPB No 5609 leads a Charing Cross-Hayes train as it calls at New Beckenham, a station distinguished perhaps only in the distance between the tracks.

REIGATE

Then: December 1964
Maunsell 'N' class 2-6-0 No 31858 arrives at Reigate over the level crossing which carries the A217 Reigate Hill Road with a train from Guildford.

Now: 16 September 1998
Thames Trains' No 165001 enters the station with the 08.37 Reading to Redhill local service. This was, and is, the limit of third rail electrification from the Redhill direction. The BR Property Board appear to be advertising the signalbox, now without its name, to let.
Andrew C. Ingham Collection/Author

Now: 3 November 1998
No 465013 is in a similar role now. The chimneys have been removed on the down side building and the hut windows boarded over, but otherwise business is as usual. *Author (2)*

ELMERS END

Then: Undated, c1955
SECR 'C' class 0-6-0 No 31280 undertakes the shunting for the engineers as the main line is slewed. This view, looking south from the station, shows the Hayes branch curving off to the left, while straight ahead is the original route of the line to Sanderstead and beyond. Lengthening platforms from 8 to 10 cars required extensions to be built, and this had to be undertaken at the south end. The then main line was thus rerouted to the left of the box, before resuming its former alignment. The locomotive is on the line which formed the Addiscombe bay.

Now: 3 November 1998
There is now only the Hayes line left, with No 465186 bringing up the rear of a departing train. The Addiscombe bay on the right has no track, just a signal! It is to be used for Croydon Tramlink. *Author's Collection/Author*

SIDCUP

Then: 29 May 1980
With the station in the distance, a
Gravesend to Charing Cross train,
formed of EPB unit No 5177, leaves
Sidcup.

Now: 3 November 1998
The bushes have grown, there are
more parked cars, and EPBs have
become Networkers. Connex
SouthEastern's No 466015 is on a
working to Charing Cross which
started at Dartford. *Author (2)*

London Underground

The Underground is a huge undertaking on which 832 million passenger journeys were made in 1997-98. This is as many passengers in a year as on the whole of National Railways. Average journey lengths at around five miles are of course much shorter, but this does give an idea of the extent of the undertaking. The Underground operates over 243 route miles, slightly more than half of which are above ground. The company owns 245 stations, though trains call at rather more since some are owned by Railtrack. A total approaching 4,000 cars, nearly all in six-, seven- or eight-car formations according to line, operate the services.

The system is made up of two distinct types of operation. The surface lines are the originals, dating from 1863. They were built by cut-and-cover methods and date from before the complexities of tunnelling for the later tube lines had been sufficiently developed. In the beginning, they also used steam traction. The following lines comprise those making up the surface operations, and the present rolling stock in use, its (nominal) year of introduction, and cars per train are also shown.

• Metropolitan	A	1960	8 cars
(4 Chesham shuttle)			
• Hammersmith & City	C	1969	6 cars
• East London	A	1960	4 cars
• Circle	C	1969	6 cars
• District (main)	D	1980	6 cars
• District (Edgware Road-Wimbledon)	C	1977	6 cars

They are characterised by rather larger rolling stock of a size commensurate with that used on National Railways, while the Metropolitan main line is in many ways more akin to the suburban operations associated with the railway companies south of the Thames.

The other 'tube' lines appeared from 1890 onwards, when electric traction and its control had been sufficiently perfected, and means of deep level access were available. Initially these were lifts, supplemented later by escalators which in many cases replaced lift installations. There were many other requirements, associated with matters such as drainage and ventilation, for instance.

Tube trains are much smaller, and with a very few minor exceptions surface and tube stock does not operate on the same lines. The tube lines and their associated rolling stock are as follows. The stock is known officially by its year of introduction, but this is often rather earlier than the time it entered revenue earning service. Cars per train are also shown.

• Bakerloo	1972	7 cars
• Central	1992	8 cars
• Jubilee	1996	6 cars
• Northern	1995	6 cars
• Piccadilly	1973	6 cars
• Victoria	1967	8 cars
• Waterloo & City	1992	4 cars

The Northern Line stock, presently in course of delivery, is replacing the 1959 and 1972 Mk1 stock in seven-car formations which operated the service before, but which were still providing most of the services in early 1999.

Train lengths vary, particularly because the lengths of platforms are not consistent on all the lines. While eight-car

1962 stock trains ran happily on the Central, the Northern was hard pushed to accommodate 7-car trains of the dimensionally identical 1959 stock. The trains themselves have to cater for dense and short-distance inner London movements (as on the Circle Line) where speed of access and egress are important, for longer distance journeys (to Amersham and Uxbridge on the Metropolitan) where a higher degree of seating comfort is called for, or for special requirements such as luggage space (Piccadilly to Heathrow). There are also different technical requirements, such as being fitted for Automatic Train Operation on the Victoria Line.

Broadly, the proportion of Underground lines in tunnel is highest in the central area and at its lowest in the outer suburbs. To some extent, this reflects the provision of railway infrastructure before housing development really got under way in those expansionary times. Only two lines are completely underground: the Waterloo & City as one of the earliest, and the Victoria as one of the newest. It may be noted that what might be termed the original Jubilee Line from Baker Street to Charing Cross and opened in 1979 is wholly underground, as is the extension to Stratford apart from the section from Canning Town northwards where it makes use of an old freight railway

formation. The longest tunnel is that of the Northern Line between East Finchley and Morden via Bank, a distance of more than 17 miles.

Service frequencies are relatively high, with many approaching 30tph. The constraints, as in National Railways, are in the junction layouts and the conflicting moves which may be needed, and matters such as different dwell time requirements at different stations. The 'bunching' of trains can take place very easily, but it has to be avoided if at all possible to keep the traffic moving freely. With negligible exceptions, other than between Wembley Park and Moor Park, the Underground is worked as a series of two-track railways. Single lines are rare; they exist on the Chesham and the Mill Hill East branches, at all the extremes of the East London Line, and also as part of the Heathrow terminal loop.

Line extensions are planned to serve Heathrow Terminal 5 if that is authorised, and more substantially for the Chelsea-Hackney scheme. The East London Line may also be extended both to the north (for which powers exist) and southwards. In the northwest, the Watford Metropolitan branch may yet be diverted to form the Croxley link and terminate instead at Watford Junction.

BAKERLOO, ELEPHANT & CASTLE

Then: 13 April 1983
The 1938 stock was a long-term provider of Bakerloo services. A train is seen arriving at the southern terminus.

Now: 17 December 1998
The 1972 stock seems likely to be an equally long-term service provider. The train indicator has been replaced and the clock has disappeared. *Author (2)*

BAKERLOO, LONDON ROAD

Then: 4 May 1985
London Road depot is of modest proportions, seen here at the beginning of the evening peak with 1959 stock entering the tunnel.

Now: 18 December 1998
Some demolition and replacement has occurred, and the 1972 stock now monopolises service provision.
Author (2)

CENTRAL, BANK

Then: July 1986
This is the eastbound platform, with a 1962 stock train for Epping arriving. Peeling paint gives the impression of a rundown railway, whatever the reality. Sir Peter Parker as BRB Chairman referred, memorably, to 'the crumbling edge of quality'.

BAKERLOO, PICCADILLY CIRCUS

Then: 13 April 1983
A 1938 stock train arrives on a northbound service; this is the point from which services in both directions can easily be viewed. The reason is the trailing crossover between the tunnels, which may be used to reverse trains arriving from the Queen's Park direction.

Now: March 1995
The station has been retiled and 'Mind the Gap' signs added along the platform edge. There is a change in the rolling stock to the 1972 variety, in corporate colours. The train is for Queen's Park. *Author (2)*

Now: 23 December 1997
The same spot with a 1992 stock train for Hainault via Newbury Park. Work has been carried out on the platform as well as the walls, showing the differences which can be achieved. Some jobs are clearly still outstanding, but that does not spoil the overall effect. It looks as though somebody cares! *Author (2)*

CENTRAL, LEYTONSTONE

Then: March 1983
The Great Eastern Railway carried straight on; London Transport built new tube tunnels for the diverging Hainault branch. The difference in dimensions explains why plans for the Chelsea-Hackney line, should that be used by surface stock, preferred Epping as a terminus to Hainault. A 1962 stock train for West Ruislip approaches from the Epping direction.

Now: 16 December 1998
1992 stock trains arrive simultaneously from both directions at the three-platformed station at Leytonstone. The additional platform, though perhaps not strictly necessary, does increase operational flexibility. *Author (2)*

CENTRAL, NORTH ACTON JUNCTION

Then: 3 October 1977
1962 stock, left, for West Ruislip and, right, from West Ruislip to Hainault. The other lines are for trains to and from Ealing Broadway. On the right is the ex-GWR main line to Birmingham.

Now: 19 December 1998
The Underground lines remain unaltered, but the Railtrack line is now reduced to single track and the box has been removed. New EWS diesel No 66032 runs light engine towards West Ruislip. *Author (2)*

CENTRAL, WOODFORD

Then: June 1990
The sad story of the Cravens units, once to be the Central Line replacement stock in the early 1960s, saw only a handful of driving motor cars constructed. Matched with a repainted 1938 stock trailer and fitted with ATO, they were put to use on the Woodford-Hainault shuttle. One such unit is seen here after arrival from Hainault.

Now: 16 December 1998
The former Great Eastern station has barely changed. A 1992 stock train arrives in the morning peak.
Author (2)

DISTRICT/PICCADILLY, CHISWICK PARK

Then: 2 July 1969
A Northfields-Lillie Bridge train runs eastwards along the District Line past Chiswick Park station behind an unidentified '57xx' 0-6-0PT. This was one of the fleet purchased by London Transport for internal use, and which outlived steam on BR by three years.

CIRCLE,
SLOANE SQUARE

Then: 5 June 1980
A C69 stock train arrives on an inner rail (or anticlockwise) working at Sloane Square. The station is unusual in being provided with escalators from the platforms to ticket office and street level. It suffered from bombing in World War 2.

Now: 19 December 1998
The C stock has been refurbished and repainted externally, presenting a quite different appearance. On the left, a D stock District Line train disappears towards Earl's Court. The station platforms have been retiled, but the area above is unchanged.
Author (2)

Now: 17 December 1998
A refurbished 1973 stock train of the Piccadilly Line passes nonstop on the centre lines, bound for Cockfosters.
D. A. Idle/Author

DISTRICT, EAST PUTNEY

Then: Undated, c1960
The line from East Putney to Wimbledon was owned by British Railways, but came under London Underground ownership from 1 April 1994. It is used on a regular basis by South West Trains' empty stock to access Wimbledon depot after the morning peak. Here, 'M7' 0-4-4T No 30241 is paired with an unidentified Light Pacific on a train of milk tanks. The train would appear to be waiting for a path over the section shared with District Line services.

Now: 4 November 1998
The platform canopies have gone and the station facilities have been updated considerably. A D stock train for Wimbledon is arriving. *Author's Collection/Author*

DISTRICT, UPMINSTER

Then: June 1986
A D stock train leaves the depot, passing the remaining water tank; it will be working a train for Wimbledon.

DISTRICT, RICHMOND

Then: 9 September 1980
Platform 7 at Richmond sees an R
stock train for Dagenham East which
will depart shortly. The tail lamp on
the back is a reminder that these
needed to be carried for back-up
purposes in case of electric lamp
failure.

Now: 8 December 1998
The D stock has been substituted, but
the station remains very much as
before. Some new development can
be seen outside the railway, but that is
about all. *Author (2)*

Now: 7 November 1998
Two D stock trains approach the
depot outlet. To some extent, the
choice of track is determined by the
platform in the station to be used for
departure. The water tank has now
gone. *Author (2)*

DISTRICT, WEST BROMPTON

Then: 30 January 1981
The C stock is used on the Edgware Road-Wimbledon service, seen here arriving at West Brompton. Both the lighting and the signing suggest that the picture could be considerably older.

Now: 17 December 1998
A D stock District Line service arrives. The station has been smartened up and will shortly be given two additional platforms. Those on the West London line for Railtrack may be glimpsed through the fencing. The prime objective is to provide additional rail services for Earl's Court Exhibition Hall. *Author (2)*

EAST LONDON, NEW CROSS GATE

Then: 13 May 1980.
The Underground looks a trifle out of place in this third rail territory, with an A stock train preparing to make the return journey to Whitechapel.

DISTRICT, WEST KENSINGTON

Then: December 1978
The District Line here, looking east from the station, is in a tight formation between roads and building. An R stock train has the destination of Ealing Broadway.

Now: 17 December 1998
A D stock train takes the route east to Upminster. The line on the left gives access to Lillie Bridge depot.
Author (2)

Now: 16 December 1998
The former BR sidings have been lifted and new housing built on their site. The A stock train and the station remain, but the new construction in the distance can hardly be termed an improvement. *Author (2)*

EAST LONDON, SOUTH OF SURREY QUAYS

Then: 1 October 1961.
The Southern Counties Touring Society's Metropolitan railtour from Stanmore to New Cross was hauled over the East London Line by Metropolitan 0-4-4T No L44. Originally, and later, this was Metropolitan No 1.

Now: 16 December 1998
A New Cross Gate train passes the same point. The site is that of the proposed junction which would take the East London Line over a new link to a possible station at Deptford Park and then onto the South London line to Peckham and beyond.
Ian Allan Library/Author

HAMMERSMITH & CITY, PADDINGTON

Then: 20 January 1962
A CO/CP stock train arrives in the then westbound platform at Paddington, the present No 13. Eastbound trains then, as now, used No 16. The intermediate platforms were used by Western Region domestic services.

HAMMERSMITH & CITY, LADBROKE GROVE

Then: 15 March 1982

A C stock train is arriving on a Hammersmith to Whitechapel service, about to pass the signalbox which was still then standing. To the right is the elevated A40(M) Westway. The Great Western built this part of the line.

Now: 17 December 1998

The scene is much the same, but the crossover has been removed as has the box. Tree growth has helped to hide the road and barriers have been installed to prevent passengers from walking off the ends of the platforms.
Author (2)

Now: 28 October 1997

No 13 is now a terminal platform used by Thames Trains, in this case No 166202 forming a Reading local service. Westbound underground trains use platform 15.
M. Mensing/Author

NORTHERN, ANGEL

Then: 12 February 1982.
The island platform at Angel was never satisfactory, but became less so as usage increased. This shows the situation as it existed from the access steps, looking southbound. The 1962 stock train is for High Barnet.

Now: 1 September 1998
The northbound platform has been diverted through a new tunnel and the old tunnel has been made over for the exclusive use of southbound trains. This is the nearest equivalent view which can now be obtained, which emphasises the spaciousness resulting. *Author (2)*

NORTHERN, MORDEN

Then: 23 September 1975
Tube trains leave Morden and plunge immediately into a cut-and-cover tunnel which quickly becomes a bored tunnel. This 1938 stock train is for Mill Hill East via Bank.

NORTHERN,
FINCHLEY CENTRAL

Then: 5 April 1976

This is a true Great Northern station, whose adaptation to the Underground era required the lowering of the platforms (though this was not carried out elsewhere). A 1972 MkI stock train for Kennington via Charing Cross is arriving in the southbound platform.

Now: 16 December 1998

A 1995 stock train arrives; changes are slight. The secondary staircase on the left, a 1960s addition, has had its roof replaced, but the character of the station remains as previously. *Author (2)*

Now: 11 November 1998

A 1959 stock train leaves Platforms 1 and 2 (they are double-sided) for the same destination. Here, as in so many other places, security has been increased, as can be seen by the fencing on the top of the surrounding wall. *Author (2)*

NORTHERN, WEST FINCHLEY

Then: May 1974
At West Finchley, one steps down into the train, in this case 1972 MkI stock which has now all been withdrawn from Northern Line service. Apart from a few splashes of mud, this picture shows how clean the aluminium finish could appear in service.

Now: 16 December 1998
The atmosphere of a wayside station still permeates; it was put together by the LNER in 1933 using bits and pieces surplus in other parts of the system. Only the ticket office has been completely renewed, though the road overbridge beyond has been reconstructed for tube clearances only. A southbound 1995 stock train is arriving. *Author (2)*

PICCADILLY, ACTON TOWN

Then: 10 May 1978
The Piccadilly was once operated with 1959 stock, and a Heathrow to Arnos Grove service is arriving at the station on the other side of the bridge, behind the photographer. This is where the lines to Ealing Broadway and to Rayners Lane separate; in the background on the right is Ealing Common depot.

Now: 19 June 1995
The Piccadilly was the first line to have a train in all-over advertising livery, for United Airlines. The 1973 stock train is seen on the Press run from Heathrow. The train ceased to carry this livery in 1998. *Author (2)*

PICCADILLY, ACTON TOWN

Then: 10 August 1978
A pair of 1973 stock trains at Acton Town. The one on the right is eastbound and the destination is incorrect. The Uxbridge train departing on this fine day has the rear cab door open; it was still occupied by a guard.

Now: 17 December 1998
The only Cravens cars to remain in LUL service are those forming the Track Recording Train, seen here with the ex-1973 stock trailer in between. *Author (2)*

PICCADILLY, HAMMERSMITH

Then: 4 October 1977
Hammersmith District & Piccadilly station has at last been totally reconstructed. The old station sees a 1973 stock train for Rayners Lane in the Piccadilly Line westbound Platform 2.

Now: 17 December 1998
The extent of the transformation can be judged from this picture. The photographer had several attempts before he achieved a refurbished train coming towards him without a westbound train or hordes of passengers obstructing the view. Hammersmith is very busy indeed!
Author (2)

VICTORIA, FINSBURY PARK

Then: 18 March 1982
The southbound platform tunnel here was formerly used by the Northern City branch. This accounts for the decided 'hump' in its centre, and the use of bricks which can be seen in the linings. A 1967 stock train for Brixton is arriving.

Now: 24 October 1997
The main change is the dot matrix indicator replacing the traditional pattern, and the corporate livery of London Underground Ltd on the train. *Author (2)*

WATERLOO & CITY, WIMBLEDON

Then: 1940
A single motor coach of the new stock was photographed on test in Wimbledon Platform 4.

WATERLOO & CITY, BANK

Then: 13 September 1983
A train of Class 487, or 1940 Waterloo & City stock, arrives at what was then a decidedly dingy terminus. With the trains then over 40 years old and no replacement in sight, the outlook was not encouraging.

Now: 28 September 1994
Trains may be cleaned in the platform at Bank outside the peak when a single platform can cope. This is one of the replacement sets, which are almost (but not quite) 1992 stock clones. *Author (2)*

Now: 15 September 1998
The present District Line users flock towards the D stock train which awaits them. It is hard to detect any changes of substance even after 58 years, though Wimbledon Theatre no longer advertises on the end wall. *Author's Collection/Author*

Docklands Light Railway

More modest than a full heavy rail or metro scheme, light rail technology enables rather cheaper schemes to be built. They may not have the capacity of more robust operations, but again that may be considered unnecessary.

The growing interest in light rail applications in London eventually found an outlet with the Docklands Light Railway. This was seen to be appropriate in an area where redevelopment was planned and transport links poor. There was also the complication of the River Thames as a southern boundary, together with the disued docks themselves.

The Docklands Light Railway (DLR) started life alongside the LTS line terminus at Fenchurch Street from a station named Tower Gateway, and thence to Limehouse, Canary Wharf (then merely a sea of mud), and to Island Gardens on the Thames facing Greenwich. That was when it opened in 1987. A branch ran via Poplar and Bow to Stratford. The whole was a response to the need to develop Docklands, but at minimum cost. In short, it was what could be built for £77 million.

The key was the use of existing, even if disused, railway formations. These comprised three-quarters of the original DLR system. Other elements were utilising the ability of rail to cross the former dock areas by relatively inexpensive bridging, and light rail technology which makes tight formations possible with both vertical and horizontal curves. The electric power was to be supplied by third rail, since, it was claimed, the site developers believed overhead equipment would look unsightly and out of keeping with the image which they wished to promote.

The initial system has now been upgraded and extended; platforms can now take a double instead of a single unit, a new signalling system has been installed with moving block, and all lines can be used in either direction. The net effect is to increase capacity, both through longer trains and each being able to follow the other closer together in safety.

An alternative in-town terminus has since been provided underground at Bank, and the line from Poplar to Beckton has been opened. The extension across the Thames from Crossharbour to Lewisham is presently under construction. Upgrading has also taken place, notably at Canary Wharf where a large covered station with three tracks and five platforms has been built, and in the approaches at West India Quay and Poplar. Many, though not all, junctions are grade separated.

Further extensions may be promoted at some stage and a link to London City Airport is likely. The DLR's third rail power supplies are of the sheathed variety with underside current collection. This means that for the foreseeable future, the railway must run on a segregated alignment, with no public access. There is thus no on-street capability.

The DLR is now operated by a homogeneous fleet of 70 cars, constructed by Bombardier BN in Bruges, Belgium.

Croydon Tramlink

The first phase of Croydon Tramlink is under construction. The approach is similar to that in Manchester, where suburban railways terminating at stations close to but not ideally sited for the city centre are linked as a light rail route across the city. In Croydon, the Wimbledon-West Croydon line forms one leg, and there is then a one-way loop round the town centre which is entirely new. Tramlink then passes East Croydon station. The line bifurcates at Sandilands, with one route serving New Addington and using in part the formation of the Elmers End to Sanderstead railway (including the tunnels), and the other proceeding along the northern part of this route. A second junction then takes some services to Birkbeck, from which point Tramlink will run alongside the (now) single track used by Connex to Beckenham Junction. Other trams will terminate at Elmers End.

This is a tramway fully compatible with on-street operation, but separated from road traffic wherever possible. Two thirds of Tramlink's route is along converted railways and disused railway routes, with less than two miles along existing roads, and five miles along new rights of way, mostly alongside roads. The total route length is 17.5 miles.

It is planned presently to run services with frequencies as follows.

Line 1	Wimbledon to Elmers End	6tph
Line 2	Croydon to Beckenham Junction	6tph
Line 3	Croydon to New Addington	9tph

This will offer 21tph in central Croydon and as far east as Sandilands. Around 40 tram stops will have platforms at 350mm above rail level, with level access to trams. These will have shelters, seating, assistance points, CCTV and displays to indicate when the next service will arrive. Extensions to serve new markets and to meet developing needs can come later. Public opening is expected around the end of 1999.

LIMEHOUSE

Then: 27 September 1983
The trackbed of what was to become the Docklands Light Railway was, quite simply, abandoned. This is the view of the western end of Limehouse BR station platforms from the DLR route. Class 302 No 312 is forming a down service.

WEST INDIA QUAY

Then: September 1987
Original car No 02 rounds the curve into the station with an Island Gardens service.

Now: 17 August 1997
From a Canary Wharf viewpoint, this picture shows the effects of doubling the railway to four tracks over this section. The tight radii which can be achieved are also shown. *Author (2)*

Now: 28 October 1998
The transformation is complete as DLR Car No 91 leads its train into Limehouse. The LT&S line can be seen behind. *Author (2)*

CANARY WHARF

Then: September 1987
The original Canary Wharf station was constructed, then demolished without being opened. Its site was marked by the DLR cars stopping, and then continuing. This view is from Heron Quays.

Now: 16 December 1998
From approximately the same viewpoint, the scale of Canary Wharf today can be judged. The arch of the station roof can just be seen.

Now: 16 December 1998
This view within the present station looks north; Car No 36 will depart away from the camera to Tower Gateway. *Author (3)*

HERON QUAYS

Then: September 1987
The DLR is open, but there is much to do before real traffic growth is experienced. The train is leaving in a northerly direction towards Canary Wharf.

Now: 16 December 1998
The platforms have been extended to take double-length trains, and matters have clearly advanced. *Author (2)*

DEVONS ROAD

Then: 25 August 1958
Devons Road was British Railways' first diesel locomotive depot; seen here are 'Jinty' ex-LMS 0-6-0T No 47517 and an 0-4-0 diesel shunter No D2907. This was one of a batch of 20 built by the North British Locomotive Co, with hydraulic transmission.

Now: 16 December 1998
The whole area has been redeveloped, and precise identification of the previous location would be of little virtue. This view is of the Devons Road DLR station looking north towards Stratford, with Car No 68 bringing up the rear of a train.
Author's Collection/Author

WEST CROYDON

Then: 21 October 1976
2EPB unit No 5654 rounds the curve off the Wimbledon branch where it joins the line from Wallington to West Croydon, alongside Waddon New Road. This view is from a footbridge linking to Wandle Park.

MORDEN ROAD

Then: March 1979
2EPB Class 416/1 No 5665 arrives
with a train for West Croydon.
Although superficially impressive, this
was in fact an unstaffed halt.
Patronage was at best 'modest'.

Now: 11 November 1998
The station has been effectively
removed, and a low platform edging
installed. The third rail has also been
taken up. *Author*

Now: 14 September 1998
The Tramlink route will cross the
Railtrack line by a new flyover, seen
here under construction; the new
footbridge visible here is already
open. *Author (2)*

Conclusions

This book is essentially a photographic look at how the railways in the London area appear today, and how they have changed in recent years. What further changes might be expected in the future?

First, the market, for whom the services are provided. London's population peaked at nearly nine million in the late 1930s, declined until the 1980s, and has now stabilised at around seven million. Stability has been experienced, too, by the Home Counties. The total population of those counties which abut directly onto London is a further 5.5 million, though as for instance in Kent, some will live as far away as the Channel ports, taking them well out of the area covered in this book.

Of the Greater London population, a quarter are less than 20 years old, and nearly 15% are over 65. There is little evidence nowadays of migration from inner to outer London as happened in the 1930s, but the population density is still highest in the inner London boroughs.

The volume of tourism, though volatile, shows a continued upward trend.

Demand for travel is however growing, and London Transport predict that even if public transport's share remains static, there will be a 20% increase in rail trips by the year 2016. For planning purposes, forecasts have to be made of where and when the growth is likely to take place, but it does indicate the scale of increased provision which may be needed.

The Trains

As the last of the Modernisation Plan equipment is replaced, the number of different types of rolling stock has shown a marked reduction. Whatever the equipment variations and the internal fittings and layout, visually there is little difference from the Class 456s on Connex SouthCentral to the Class 321s on Silverlink and Great Eastern, or the Class 322s built for Stansted Express. Likewise, the Class 165/166 family of diesel units on Chiltern Railways and Thames Trains is very similar to the later Class 365 electrics on WAGN and Connex South Eastern or the Class 465/6s, also on Connex South Eastern.

On the other hand, Train Operating Companies wish to promote their own services, and distinguish them in the public's mind from those of others. One way is the adoption of company liveries, albeit that this is a relatively long drawn out process and takes time to implement. Another, where brand-new stock is concerned, is to apply an external treatment to reflect a personalised approach. The Class 332 units supplied to BAA for the Heathrow services are not reminiscent of any others presently in service, and the Class 168s for the Chiltern Express services to Birmingham are also 'different'. Other new trains have yet to enter service at the time of writing, but several multiple-unit types are nearing completion.

Internal treatments seem already to be promoting a more spacious layout, with the 3+2 seating in most ex-NSE standard class accommodation now sometimes giving way to 2+2 arrangements. Within the British loading gauge, to offer five across *and* an adequate gangway does tend to compromise comfort, and this becomes increasingly important when the trains are used for longer journeys. Seat pitch is a related issue, but the net effect of providing more spacious car interiors is that a seating capacity of 84 in a 20m vehicle quickly drops to below 70. With a full load, as is often the case on commuter services, either more trains have to be provided, or more people have to stand, albeit more comfortably. More trains means more costs, which have to be remunerated somehow, and higher fares are the only real answer. Do we have the quality and price mix right at the moment, or is there an opportunity for increasing both of them?

On the Underground, plans are under way for new generation rolling stock, starting with that needed to replace the 1967 stock on the Victoria Line. Early ideas included the following:
• more spacious trains in the deep tube lines, with small wheels and overhead power supply, creating extra headroom within the cars;
• articulated trains with no effective division between cars, to increase space and enable more even loading, with fully automatic operation to allow staff to patrol the whole train for security reasons;
• air-conditioning, which is expected increasingly as it becomes more common in cars and on National Railways; and
• measures to reduce internal noise levels.
Another issue for National Railways, as well as the Underground, is the effect of the new Regulations made under the Disability Discrimination Act. These require the provision of access for wheelchairs and accommodation for them on the train. And while there is no statutory requirement, the accommodation of bicycles is another difficult issue since it reduces the space available for paying passengers. Should bicycles be charged on the basis of the space which they occupy and, if not, why not?

Finally, on longer-distance services particularly, the provision

ELMERS END

Then: 1948
A vintage view of a Southern 3SUB, unit No 1753, in the up bay platform used for the shuttle trains to Addiscombe.

of catering facilities can either be by trolley at minimal capital cost and only small space requirements, or by the traditional dining car arrangements with or without a separate buffet counter. Railway systems throughout the world find it difficult to solve this conundrum, and innovative ideas may well be forthcoming. There may also be new ideas for on-board entertainment; entertainment screens on the back of the seat in front are a reality on some aircraft used for long-distance travel.

The Infrastructure

In recent times, rail traffic has been growing, both passenger and freight. While all train service providers are subject to the changes in travel habits and the economic activity levels which result from the ups and downs of the national economy, there are increasing signs that spare line capacity is less available than might be thought. Much effort has gone into removing capacity that can be considered spare in recent years, thus eliminating its maintenance costs as well as the need for renewal.

One example is junction simplification. If a double-track splits into two directions and each also double-track, the minimum requirement is for a crossover between the two tracks of the main line, a turnout to the branch, and a second turnout restoring the double track arrangement on that branch. But the down side is the speed at which the junction can be taken, and the reduced ability to perform more than one move at the same time.

Railtrack's Network Management Statement lists and discusses locations at which capacity problems are already being felt or are anticipated in the future. It is certainly the wish of government to see more traffic on rail, both passenger and freight, but this does have to be accommodated.

It is essential that capacity problems, whether on the West Coast main line, or the East Coast main line, or on the North or West London lines which tie the capital's network together, should be resolved if growth of rail traffic is to come. And while there may be a general will to see more traffic on rail, this does not actually produce it, nor the business case for making the necessary investment.

This then leads to the priority that each type of rail traffic might have. Do the passenger businesses by definition have priority over freight, or not? Within the passenger businesses, is there some sort of pecking order between main line expresses and suburban services, and who presides as judge on the claim that each should have first call on the capacity which exists at any one time? To use a London Underground example, of course there is plenty of spare capacity available on the Central Line to take people to the City. Really? Yes, provided an arrival time at Bank between 01.00 and 05.00 is acceptable. (For this

purpose, the night-time occupations for engineering work are ignored.) Travel is time sensitive, and this can apply equally to freight traffic where 'just-in-time' supply chains are in operation.

With passenger traffic, most service providers have to comply with their formal Passenger Service Requirements (PSR) as stated in their contracts with the Franchising Director, and this is one of the determinants of priorities. There is however by definition no PSR for services provided on a competitive basis, or otherwise in addition to the PSR.

Overall though, consideration of the use made of various parts of the network, and how this could perhaps be extended, is opportune. This does not necessarily mean running more trains, if traffic growth can be accommodated using longer trains or larger capacity vehicles. This could mean increasing the loading gauge on selected routes to allow piggyback operation for freight, or double-deck operation for passenger traffic. It would undoubtedly be a costly exercise, but it might be possible to make a sound financial case for it. As always, how robust are the forecasts of growth, and what other alternatives are available?

On London Underground, the present emphasis is on the splitting of the organisation between operating and infrastructure companies and the method by which reorganisation will be achieved. It is also a priority to get the Jubilee Line Extension fully operational. Major new investment schemes seem unlikely to go ahead until such matters are resolved.

The reality is that investment in railway infrastructure is not for the faint-hearted, and neither is it a short-term exercise. But there can be enormous and real benefits. On a large scale, one has to be certain as to what one is trying to achieve; hence the government's proposals for a Strategic Railway Authority. As a senior railway engineer once said to the author, 'We have been building railways for a long time now, and there aren't many technical problems which we haven't found a way of overcoming. But for any new scheme we do need to study the land take required, how long the construction period will be, and how much it will all cost. It is then up to the project sponsors to say whether or not the scheme is acceptable.'

The effects of the Railways Act 1993 on the evolution of National Railways in the London area and elsewhere will continue to develop for many years to come, subject of course to the impact of new legislation setting up the Mayor for London and that which follows the 1998 White Paper on Transport. What does seem to be certain is that a 'Now' photographic exercise carried out in perhaps 15 years time, after all the present franchises have expired and have been relet on whatever terms seem appropriate at the time, or rescinded in favour of some other method of service provision, will be recording a substantially different railway.

Now: 3 November 1998
The goods yard has become a car park and the track has gone — but it is still Platform 1! It is understood that the track level will be raised to adopt the present platform height and thus enable straightforward interchange with Connex SouthEastern services.
Author's Collection/Author

Appendix I

Train operating companies at each London terminal, 1998-9

Fenchurch Street	LTS Rail
Liverpool Street	Anglia Railways, Great Eastern Railway, West Anglia Great Northern Railway, LTS Rail
Moorgate GN&C	West Anglia Great Northern Railway
King's Cross	Great North Eastern Railway, West Anglia Great Northern Railway
Farringdon, Moorgate	Thameslink
St Pancras	Midland Main Line
Euston	Virgin West Coast, Virgin CrossCountry, Silverlink Train Services, ScotRail Railways, North Western Trains
Marylebone	Chiltern Railways
Paddington	Great Western Trains, Thames Trains, Virgin CrossCountry, Chiltern Railways, Heathrow Express
Victoria	Gatwick Express, Connex South Central, Connex South Eastern
Waterloo	South West Trains, Wales & West, Eurostar
London Bridge (Brighton)	Connex South Central
Charing Cross	Connex South Eastern, Connex South Central
Cannon Street	Connex South Eastern
Blackfriars	Thameslink, Connex South Eastern

Note: Great Eastern, Great Western and North Western are operated by the FirstGroup with the prefix First before the name.

Appendix II

New stations since 1960

Excluding those on new lines, and interchanges with others such as the new Canada Water station on both the Jubilee and East London Lines, new stations consist of the following:

1960	Southbury	between Edmonton Green and Cheshunt
1960	Theobalds Grove	between Edmonton Green and Cheshunt
1960	Turkey Street	between Edmonton Green and Cheshunt
1966	Garston	on the Watford-St Albans branch
1974	Basildon	between Laindon and Pitsea
1979	West Ham (NLL)	between Stratford and Canning Town
1980	Hackney Central	between Canonbury and Stratford
1980	Hackney Wick	between Canonbury and Stratford
1982	Watton-at-Stone	between Hertford North and Stevenage
1982	Watford Stadium	on the moribund Croxley Green branch
1983	Dalston Kingsland	between Canonbury and Stratford
1985	Homerton	between Canonbury and Stratford
1986	Welham Green	between Brookmans Park and Hatfield
1988	How Wood	on the Watford-St Albans branch
1988	Martins Heron	between Ascot and Bracknell
1995	Chafford Hundred	between Ockendon and Grays
1999	West Ham (LTS)	between Limehouse and Barking
1999	Luton Airport Parkway	between Harpenden and Luton
1999	West Brompton (WLL)	between Kensington Olympia and Clapham Junction

To the above may be added stations which have been substantially resited:

1973	Stevenage (on a site much nearer the New Town, replaced the original Stevenage).
1981	Blackhorse Road (to provide interchange with the Victoria Line)
1985	Eltham (replaced Eltham Well Hall and Eltham Park, A2 road improvements).
1990	City Thameslink (replaced Holborn Viaduct, on a new alignment for Thameslink).
1992	Hillingdon (replaced the original Hillingdon, result of the A40(M) diversion).
1999	Canning Town (to provide interchange with the Jubilee Line and Docklands Light Railway).

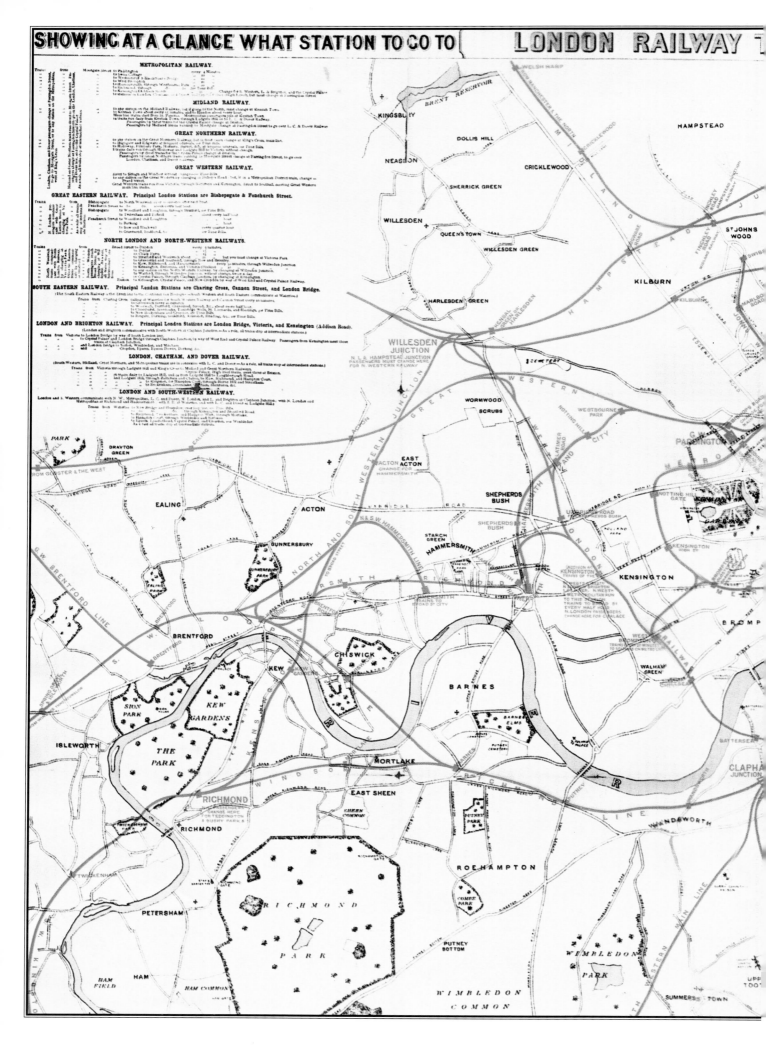